AutoCAD
2018
TRAINING GUIDE

BY
LINKAN SAGAR

BPB PUBLICATIONS
20 Ansari Road, Daryaganj, New Delhi-110002

FIRST EDITION 2018

Copyright © BPB Publication, INDIA

ISBN: 978-93-86551-87-0

Distributors:

BPB PUBLICATIONS
20, Ansari Road, Darya Ganj
New Delhi-110002
Ph: 23254990/23254991

BPB BOOK CENTRE
376 Old Lajpat Rai Market,
Delhi-110006
Ph: 23861747

COMPUTER BOOK CENTRE
12, Shrungar Shopping Centre,
M.G.Road, Bengaluru–560001
Ph: 25587923/25584641

DECCAN AGENCIES
4-3-329, Bank Street,
Hyderabad-500195
Ph: 24756967/24756400

MICRO MEDIA
Shop No. 5, Mahendra Chambers,
150 DN Rd. Next to Capital Cinema,
V.T. (C.S.T.) Station, MUMBAI-400 001
Ph: 22078296/22078297

Published by Manish Jain for BPB Publications, 20, Ansari Road, Darya Ganj, New Delhi-110002 and Printed by Repro India Pvt Ltd, Mumbai

Preface

My vigorous effort towards the understanding of students & their problems in AutoCAD will probably solve after my attempt for this book. So far my last book 'AUTOCAD 2017 TRAINING GUIDE' has been a success for my beloved readers. I have tried to be more eloquent this time with better projects and easy language. This book carries a lot for you if you are with AutoCAD for the 1st time. Book is extremely simple to understand and can enlighten you with the basics fundamentals of AutoCAD. The main objective of writing this book after getting inspired from my last edition is to make students enthusiastic about learning the concepts of AutoCAD. I wish you a great future in designing.

"DESIGNING THE WORLD"

Acknowledgements

While writing this book, I was constantly supported and guided by many wonderful people around me. Their extended support will always be priceless for me. My mother Mrs. Archana Sagar, is a woman of Substance. Like any other mother in the world, her unconditional support, caring nature, never ending Faith in me, and motivation encouraged me to finally realize that I can transfer my knowledge through writing to various other people who seek the same knowledge. And this is how my book writing started. Many thanks to my wife Mansi Sagar, who is a wonderful partner, she not only understands my dreams and aspirations but is equally trying to internalize and live it up with me. It's wonderful how she took all the responsibilities on her own shoulder to give me space and comfort so that I can dedicate more time for writing. She stands strong with me in all the highs and lows of my life. These two women are the source of continuous energy that keeps me going. My book is all about technical skills precision and perfection in the engineering field. I am highly obliged to My Mentor Mr. Manoj Kumar Dwivedi, for his guidance in Design Approvals throughout my writing, His sharp technical & analytical skills and in-depth knowledge of the subject matter, amazed me. It is due to his continuous guidance I could write a book of relevance and great content. I am equally thankful to Ms. Jyoti Chhabra, who took the responsibility of proof reading my writing and editing to make it grammatically sound and graspable. Her expertise and great insight helped a lot in shaping my book contents and put my thoughts in appropriate words. My sincerest thanks are also due to all the other people for their invaluable help in compiling this Volume. Also I feel equally indebted to BPB Publication which has given me opportunity to collaborate and taken responsibility to publish my books.

Contents

CHAPTER-1

Introduction

WHAT IS AutoCAD ?

Autodesk Company who develop a software named AutoCAD, stands for Autodesk's Computer aided design. It's a drafting and designing software. There are several software for drafting and designing available in market, Out of them The AutoCAD is best, because it Works on co-ordinate system, that help's in survey drawing and drafting.

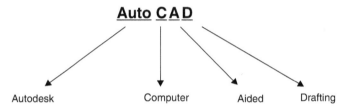

Auto **C A** D

Autodesk Computer Aided Drafting

HISTORY OF AutoCAD?

AutoCAD was Came in concept during 1977, and it's first commercial release was in 1979 with the name Interact CAD. Later on Autodesk Company develop it and Release in 1982 for Microcomputer. Gradually the lighter version for small PC and Notebook were release. In 2010 AutoCAD 360 app was released for mobile.

OLD AutoCAD 1982   **New AutoCAD 2018**

USAGE OF AutoCAD

AutoCAD is used for 2D and 3D design, mostly for Civil, Mechanical, Electrical, Interior & Architecture domain. You can design & draw layout, building plan, mechanical part etc. This software is very popular among small to large scale Companies.

AutoCAD stands for Automatic Computer Aided Design.

1. As an Architectural planning tool.

2. As an Engineering drafting tool.

3. As a Graphic design tool.

4. In the fashion industry.

5. As an industrial design tool.

WHAT IS NEW IN AutoCAD 2018?

Every year AutoCAD new version is released with some new tools and feature as well as carrying previous feature.

AutoCAD 2018 is also released with some new and enhanced feature.

For ex.

- PDF import
- External file references
- Object selection
- Text to Mtext
- User interface
- Share design views
- High-resolution monitor support
- AutoCAD mobile app

WHAT IS WORKSPACE ?

Workspace provides us a platform for carrying out our work with definite sets of Menus, toolbars, palettes, which are displayed according to the work space selected. A workspace may also display the ribbon toolbar; it is a distinct palette with task specific Control panels. One can easily switch between workspaces. We are aided with the following task based Workspaces in AutoCAD 2018:

- 2D Drafting & Annotation
- 3D Modeling
- 3D Basic
- AutoCAD Classic

Say for example, if we have to create 3D models, we can use the 3D modeling Workspace, which provides us only 3D-related toolbars, menus, and palettes. And Hides the other interface items that we do not need for 3D modeling, thus maximizing the screen area available for our work. Depending upon our drawing requirement, we can modify a selected workspace with our choices of tools and pallets and save it as a new workspace with a different name for easy access in future.

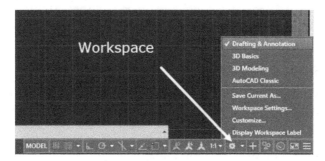

Workspace

- **2D Drafting & Annotation**

- **3D Modeling**

- **3D Basic**

- **AutoCAD Classic**

CHAPTER – 2

Overview

WELCOME SCREEN

It is the first time that Autodesk AutoCAD has introduced a welcome screen in its version of 2018. In this version when we open the AutoCAD we get to see a welcome screen. The welcome screen provides easy learning, starting, and exploring AutoCAD. In this screen, we will get to see two different types of tab at the bottom namely LEARN and CREATE. In this version, we can add the number of new tab according to our requirement. When we choose to add a new tab, we get Create page by default.

■ What is NEW TAB CREATE?

In this tab, we will have three columns providing us options to proceed as per our Requirement. Three columns namely Get Started, Recent Documents and Get connected. The name of columns gives us a notion of its use. Let's begin with "GET STARTED" it is for starting a fresh new drawing page, or we can work upon our previously drawn file by browsing the folder. Next is "RECENT DOCUMENT" this column provides instant access to the file that we lastly worked upon in AutoCAD. And finally "GET CONNECTED" provides us web access to Autodesk 360 and also shows us notifications (if any) regarding AutoCAD.

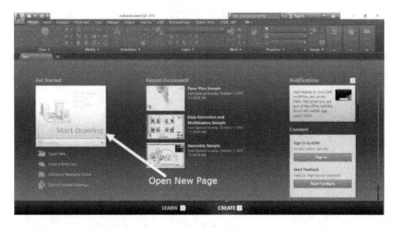

■ What is NEW TAB LEARN?

Day by day increasing use of AutoCAD is attracting new users, Keeping this in mind AutoCAD 2018 comes with a learn tab providing its new users easy learning via its three columns namely:

What's new, Getting Started Videos and TIP/Online Resources.

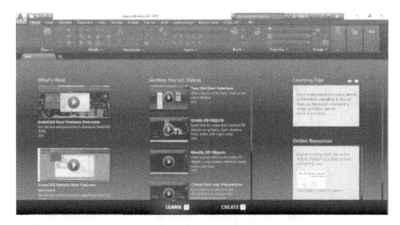

GUI (Graphical User Interface) Overview

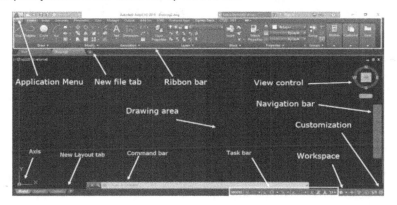

MOUSE USE

Left button of mouse is used to CLICK and Right button is used for ENTER. To move the AutoCAD page press the scroll button and move the mouse. If you have to do zoom in and zoom out the page just revolve the scroll button.

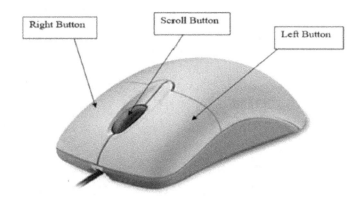

DIFFERENCE BETWEEN COMMAND WORK & VISUAL WORK

AutoCAD provide two mode of operation, first is Command based work and another is visual work.

When you work using GUI (Graphical User Interface), consider an example of using tools icon this is visual work and when you do same thing using command that is visual work. For Example if you have to draw line using command write L in command bar and press ENTER, And if you want to draw using visual click on line Icon.

Visual tools   **Commands**

 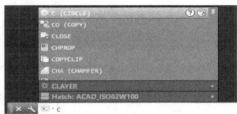

COORDINATE SYSTEM WITH LINE COMMAND

Our AutoCAD page is based on graphical coordinate system that constitutes three axis viz. x, y, z. As we know these three axis starts from a point origin (0, 0, 0) one in the vertical direction, next horizontal and the last parallel to the page. Moving forward in any of the axes increases the value of the coordinate in that axis.

We can draw using any of the three coordinates system given below:

■ Absolute Coordinate System (X, Y)

We use absolute coordinate system when we know the precise distance of x coordinate and y coordinate from the origin.

Step 1: Command: L ⏎

Step 2: Specify first point: 0, 0 ⏎

Step 3: Specify next point or [Undo]: 10, 0 ⏎

Step 4: Specify next point or [Undo]: 10, 2 ⏎

Step 5: Specify next point or [Close/Undo]: 8, 2 ⏎

Step 6: Specify next point or [Close/Undo]: 8, 5 ⏎

Step 7: Specify next point or [Close/Undo]: 6, 5 ⏎

Step 8: Specify next point or [Close/Undo]: 6, 7 ⏎

Step 9: Specify next point or [Close/Undo]: 4, 7 ⏎

Step 10: Specify next point or [Close/Undo]: 4, 5 ⏎

Step 11: Specify next point or [Close/Undo]: 2, 5 ⏎

Step 12: Specify next point or [Close/Undo]: 2, 2 ⏎

Step 13: Specify next point or [Close/Undo]: 0, 2 ⏎

Step 14: Specify next point or [Close/Undo]: C ⏎

(**Note:** Enter command and then follow instructions.)

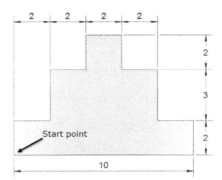

■ Relative Rectangular Coordinate System (@X, Y)

We use this coordinate system when we have a relative distance, i.e., distance of the next point with respect to previous drawn point.

Step 1: Command: L `Enter`

Step 2: Specify first point: Pick any point `Enter`

Step 3: Specify next point or [Undo]: @2, 0 `Enter`

Step 4: Specify next point or [Undo]: @0, -2 `Enter`

Step 5: Specify next point or [Close/Undo]: @3, 0 `Enter`

Step 6: Specify next point or [Close/Undo]: @0, 3 `Enter`

Step 7: Specify next point or [Close/Undo]: @5, 0 `Enter`

Step 8: Specify next point or [Close/Undo]: @0, 3 `Enter`

Step 9: Specify next point or [Close/Undo]: @-3, 0 `Enter`

Step 10: Specify next point or [Close/Undo]: @0, 3 `Enter`

Step 11: Specify next point or [Close/Undo]: @-3, 0 `Enter`

Step 12: Specify next point or [Close/Undo]: @0, -1 `Enter`

Step 13: Specify next point or [Close/Undo]: @-2, 0 `Enter`

Step 14: Specify next point or [Close/Undo]: C `Enter`

(Note: Use always @ Symbols for relative rectangle.)

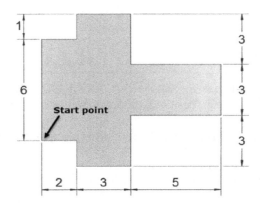

■ Relative Polar Coordinate System (@ distance < angle)

We use relative polar coordinate system when we have a relative distance and angle of a point to draw with respect to the previous point. The use of angle is compulsory in this coordinate system which is measured in Anti clock direction, taking towards the right.

Step 1: Command: L [Enter]

Step 2: Specify first point: Pick any point [Enter]

Step 3: Specify next point or [Undo]: @30<0 [Enter]

Step 4: Specify next point or [Undo]: @30<-60 [Enter]

Step 5: Specify next point or [Undo]: @30<60 [Enter]

Step 6: Specify next point or [Close/Undo]: @30<0 [Enter]

Step 7: Specify next point or [Close/Undo]: @30<120 [Enter]

Step 8: Specify next point or [Close/Undo]: @30<60 [Enter]

Step 9: Specify next point or [Close/Undo]: @30<180 [Enter]

Step 10: Specify next point or [Close/Undo]: @30<120 [Enter]

Step 11: Specify next point or [Close/Undo]: @30<240 [Enter]

Step 12: Specify next point or [Close/Undo]: @30<180 [Enter]

Step 13: Specify next point or [Close/Undo]: @30<-60 [Enter]

Step 14: Specify next point or [Close/Undo]: C [Enter]

(Note: Use always @ Symbols for relative and < for angle)

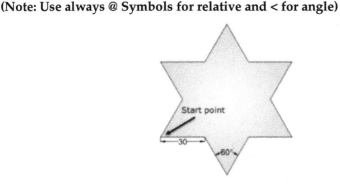

ZOOM AND EXTENTS

Use the mouse scroll bar to ZOOM IN ZOOM OUT the drawing created on AutoCAD page, in case scroll does not support then type z in command bar and press enter to zoom.

If created drawing have unexpected size then zoom it and extend after.

Step 1: Command: Z [Enter]

Step 2: Zoom [All Center Dynamic Extents Previous Scale Window Object]: E [Enter]

| Before Zoom Command | After Zoom Command |

If you want select any other option Like:-

```
1   2   3   4   5   6   7   8
```

1. **All**

   It is used to only for gird limits.

   Step 1: Z `Enter.` Then A `Enter.`

2. **Center**

   It is used as s center point and a magnification value or a height.

   Step 1: Z `Enter.` Then C `Enter.`

   Step 2: Pick center point

   Step 3: Specify height

3. **Dynamic**

   Pans and zooms using a rectangular view box. The view box represents your view, which you can shrink or enlarge and move around the drawing. Positioning and sizing the view box pans or zooms to fill the viewport with the view inside the view box. Not available in perspective projection.

   Step 1: Z `Enter.` Then D `Enter.`

   Step 2: Specify the area again `Enter.`

4. Extents

It is used to zoom all objects.

Step 1: Z [Enter,] Then E [Enter,]

5. Previous

Zooms to display the previous view. You can restore up to 10 previous views.

Step 1: Z [Enter,] Then P [Enter,]

6. Scale

It is used to zoom scale like 2 times, 3 times.

Step 1: Z [Enter,] Then S [Enter,]

Step 2: 3x (for 3 times zoom) [Enter,]

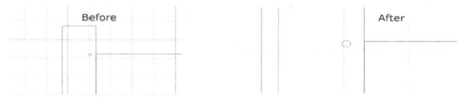

7. Window

Zooms to display an area by rectangle window.

Step 1: Z [Enter,] Then W [Enter,]

Step 2: Select window area corner to corner.

8. **Object**

    It is used to zoom select object.

Step 1: Z [Enter] Then O [Enter]

Step 2: Select object [Enter]

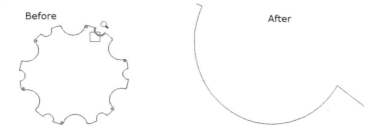

Before   After

REGEN

Usually and mostly during zoom in and zoom out of AutoCAD pages, it's not working properly, Or when you move the page it refrain to move, Or when you create circle and want to view by zoom in it appear like polygon. So, to resolve these problem use the REGAN command to overcome such type of problem.

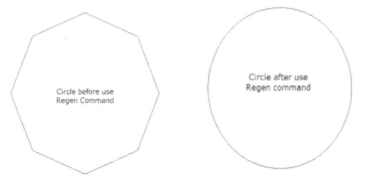

Circle before use Regen Command   Circle after use Regen command

PRACTICE DRAWING #1

Use Absolute coordinate system

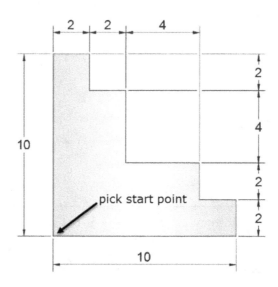

Step 1: Command: L [Enter]

Step 2: Specify first point: 0, 0 [Enter]

Step 3: Specify next point or [Undo]: 10, 0 [Enter]

Step 4: Specify next point or [Undo]: 10, 2 [Enter]

Step 5: Specify next point or [Close/Undo]: 8, 2 [Enter]

Step 6: Specify next point or [Close/Undo]: 8, 4 [Enter]

Step 7: Specify next point or [Close/Undo]: 4, 4 [Enter]

Step 8: Specify next point or [Close/Undo]: 4, 8 [Enter]

Step 9: Specify next point or [Close/Undo]: 2, 8 [Enter]

Step 10: Specify next point or [Close/Undo]: 2, 10 [Enter]

Step 11: Specify next point or [Close/Undo]: 0, 10 [Enter]

Step 12: Specify next point or [Close/Undo]: C [Enter]

PRACTICE DRAWING #2

Use Relative rectangle coordinate system

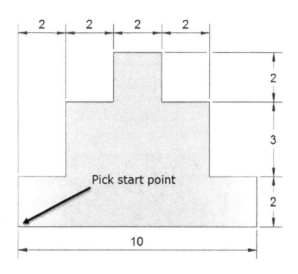

Step 1: Command: L `Enter,`

Step 2: Specify first point: Pick any point `Enter,`

Step 3: Specify next point or [Undo]: @10, 0 `Enter,`

Step 4: Specify next point or [Undo]: @0, 2 `Enter,`

Step 5: Specify next point or [Close/Undo]: @-2, 0 `Enter,`

Step 6: Specify next point or [Close/Undo]: @0, 3 `Enter,`

Step 7: Specify next point or [Close/Undo]: @-2, 0 `Enter,`

Step 8: Specify next point or [Close/Undo]: @0, 2 `Enter,`

Step 9: Specify next point or [Close/Undo]: @-2, 0 `Enter,`

Step 10: Specify next point or [Close/Undo]: @0, -2 `Enter,`

Step 11: Specify next point or [Close/Undo]: @-2, 0 `Enter,`

Step 12: Specify next point or [Close/Undo]: @0, -3 `Enter,`

Step 13: Specify next point or [Close/Undo]: @-2, 0 `Enter,`

Step 14: Specify next point or [Close/Undo]: C `Enter,`

CHAPTER – 3

Draw Tools

What do you mean by LINE

Line command is straight continuous joining points without any curve and infinite if we do not mention its start point and end point.

Step 1: **Ribbon**: Home tab ➤ Draw panel ➤Line

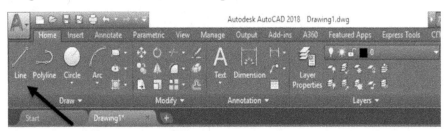

OR

Command: L [Enter]

Step 2: Specify first point: Pick any point

Step 3: Specify next point: 4 [Enter]

(Give Direction then specify distance)

Step 4: Specify next point or [Undo]: 1.5 [Enter]

Step 5: Specify next point or [Close/Undo]: 4 [Enter]

Step 6: Specify next point or [Close/Undo]: 3 [Enter]

Step 7: Specify next point or [Close/Undo]: 1 [Enter]

Step 8: Specify next point or [Close/Undo]: 2 [Enter]

Step 9: Specify next point or [Close/Undo]: 3 [Enter]

Step 10: Specify next point or [Close/Undo]: 3 [Enter]

Step 11: Specify next point or [Close/Undo]: 4 [Enter]

Step 12: Specify next point or [Close/Undo]: 3 [Enter]

Step 13: Specify next point or [Close/Undo]: 2.5 [Enter]

Step 14: Specify next point or [Close/Undo]: 1.5 [Enter]

Step 15: Specify next point or [Close/Undo]: 2.5 [Enter]

Step 16: Specify next point or [Close/Undo]: 1 [Enter]

(**Note:** Use again Enter or Esc for finish line command)

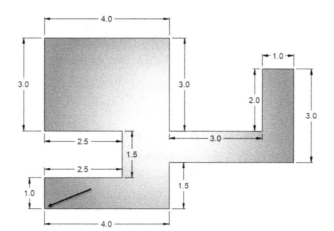

What do you mean by PLINE

Command Pline stands for polyline and is same as line and created in the same way as line is created but it requires 1st and 2nd endpoints. It is an object but may have different segments. In polyline, each segment can be given required width and can be also given different width to the start and end of the polyline.

Step 1: Ribbon: Home tab ➤ Draw panel ➤ Pline (polyline)

OR

Command: PL Enter, Enter,

Step 2: Specify first point: 1, 1 Enter,

Step 3: PLINE Specify next point or [Arc Halfwidth Length Undo Width]: 2, 2 Enter,

Step 4: PLINE Specify next point or [Arc Halfwidth Length Undo Width]: 3 Enter, (give right side direction then enter value)

Step 5: PLINE Specify next point or [Arc Close Halfwidth Length Undo Width]: 1 Enter, (give down side direction then enter value)

Step 6: PLINE Specify next point or [Arc Close Halfwidth Length Undo Width]: 2 Enter, (give right side direction then enter value)

Step 7: PLINE Specify next point or [Arc Close Halfwidth Length Undo Width]: @2<45 Enter,

Step 8: PLINE Specify next point or [Arc Close Halfwidth Length Undo Width]: 3 ⏎ (give up side direction then enter value)

Step 9: PLINE Specify next point or [Arc Close Halfwidth Length Undo Width]: 1 ⏎ (give left side direction then enter value)

Step 10: PLINE Specify next point or [Arc Close Halfwidth Length Undo Width]: 1 ⏎ (give up side direction then enter value)

Step 11: PLINE Specify next point or [Arc Close Halfwidth Length Undo Width]: 3 ⏎ (give left side direction then enter value)

Step 12: PLINE Specify next point or [Arc Close Halfwidth Length Undo Width]: 1.4 ⏎ (give down side direction then enter value)

Step 13: PLINE Specify next point or [Arc Close Halfwidth Length Undo Width]: 2.6 ⏎ (give left side direction then enter value)

Step 14: PLINE Specify next point or [Arc Close Halfwidth Length Undo Width]: C ⏎ (C for close line)

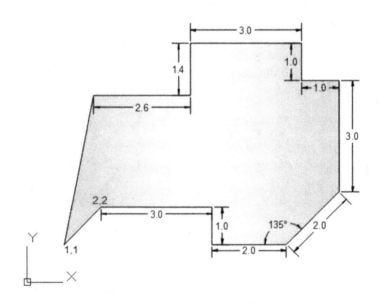

If you want select any other option Like:

1. **Arc**

   It is used to create Arc. Arc is a part of circle.

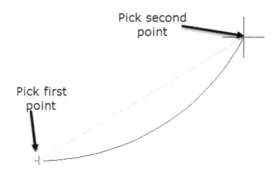

2. **Halfwidth**

   It is used to change the line width. But it is two directional.

3. **Length**

   It is used to create a line with same direction.

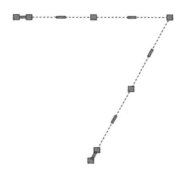

4. **Undo**

   It is used to reverse step.

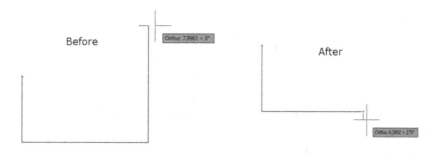

5. **Width**

    It is used to Change the line width.

What do you mean by XLINE

It is a command which is infinite and used to create construction line, reference line and for trimming boundaries.

Step 1: Ribbon: Home tab ➤ Draw panel ➤ Xline

 Then

OR

Command: XL [Enter,]

Step 2: Specify a point or [Hor Ver Ang Bisect Offset]: **Use one of the points fixing methods or enter an option**

Step 3: Specify through point: **Pick through point**

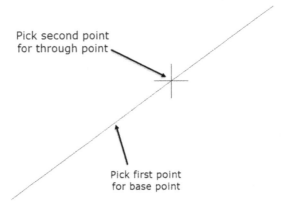

Pick second point
for through point

Pick first point
for base point

If you want to select any other option Like:

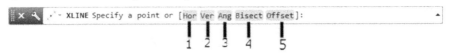

1. **Hor**

    Creates a horizontal xline passing through a selected point.

2. **Ver**

   Creates a Vertical xline passing through a selected point.

3. **Ang**

   Creates a xline at a specified angle.

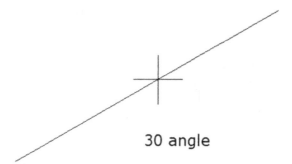

30 angle

4. **Bisect**

   It creates a xline that passes through a selected angle vertex and bisects the angle between first and second line.

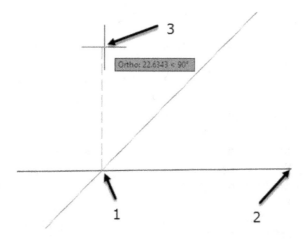

5. **Offset Distance**
    Specifies the distance the xline is offset from the selected object.

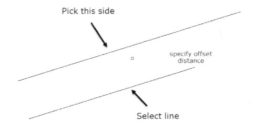

Pick this side

specify offset
distance

Select line

What do you mean by SPLINE

It is a command for making smooth curves and can be constructed along specific points.

Step 1: **Ribbon:** Home tab ➤ Draw panel ➤ Spline

 then

OR

Command: SPL [Enter]

Step 2: SPLINE Specify first point or [Method Knots Object]: pick point 1

Step 3: Specify Enter next point or [start Tangency toLerance]: pick point 2

Step 4: Specify Enter next point or [end Tangency toLerance Undo]: pick point 3

Step 5: Specify Enter next point or [end Tangency toLerance Undo Close]: pick point 4

Step 6: Specify Enter next point or [end Tangency toLerance Undo Close]: pick point 5

Step 7: Specify Enter next point or [end Tangency toLerance Undo Close]: pick point 6

Step 8: Specify Enter next point or [end Tangency toLerance Undo Close]: pick point 7

Step 9: Specify Enter next point or [end Tangency toLerance Undo Close]: pick point 8

Step 10: Specify Enter next point or [end Tangency toLerance Undo Close]: pick point 9

Step 11: Specify Enter next point or [end Tangency toLerance Undo Close]: pick point 10

Step 12: Specify Enter next point or [end Tangency toLerance Undo Close]: C

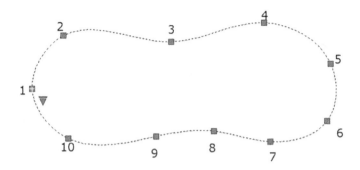

If you select any other option Like:

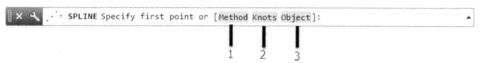

1. **Method**

   It is used to create Fit and CV spline.

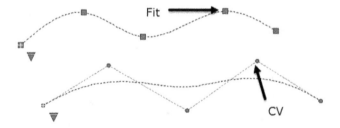

2. **Knots**

   It is used to create knots.

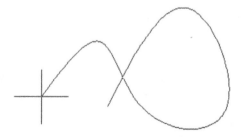

3. **Method**

   It is used to create Fit and CV spline.

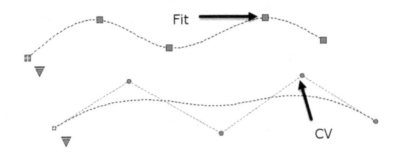

What do you mean by CIRCLE

It is a command by which we can make a curved line joined in the end having equal distance from the center point. Circle help us to create two-way normal. But in AutoCAD there are three ways to create Circle. One is by specifying the radius and second by specifying Diameter. Besides this 2point, 3point, and tan tan radius. Here we have five ways to create Circle.

Step 1:   Ribbon: Home tab ➢ Draw panel ➢Circle

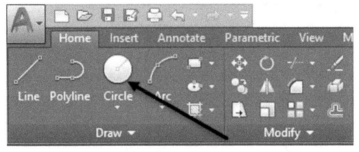

OR

Command: C Enter,

Step 2:   Specify center point for circle or [3P/ 2P/ Ttr (tan tan radius)]: **Pick a point**

Step 3:   Specify radius of circle or [Diameter]: **10**

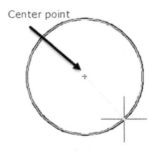

Circle diameter

Command: C

  Step 1: Specify center point for circle or [3P/ 2P/ Ttr (tan tan radius)]: **Specify a point**

  Step 2: Specify radius of circle or [Diameter]: **D** [Enter.]

  Step 3: Specify diameter of circle: **20** [Enter.]

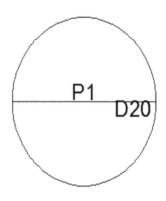

3P (Three point)

Draws a circle based on three points on the circumference.

Command: C [Enter.]

  Step 1: Specify center point for circle or [3P/ 2P/ Ttr (tan tan radius)]: **3P** [Enter.]

  Step 2: Specify first point on circle: **Specify a point (1)**

  Step 3: Specify second point on circle: **Specify a point (2)**

  Step 4: Specify third point on circle: **Specify a point (3)**

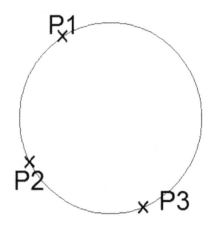

2P (Two point)

Draws a circle based on two endpoints of the diameter.

Command: C [Enter]

   Step 1: Specify center point for circle or [3P/ 2P/ Ttr (tan tan radius)]: **2P** [Enter]

   Step 2: Specify fxirst endpoint of circle's diameter: **Specify a point**

   Step 3: Specify second endpoint of circle's diameter: **Specify a point**

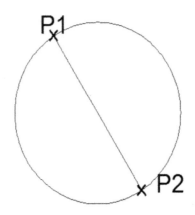

TTR (Tangent, Tangent, Radius)

Draws a circle with a specified radius tangent to two objects.

Command: C [Enter]

   Step 1: Specify center point for circle or [3P/ 2P/ Ttr (tan tan radius)]: **T** [Enter]

   Step 2: Specify point on object for first tangent of circle: **Select a line**

   Step 3: Specify point on object for second tangent of circle: **Select a line**

   Step 4: Specify radius of circle < *current*>: **Enter radius**

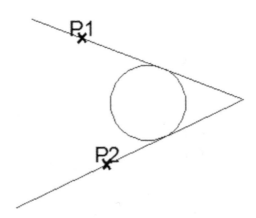

What do you mean by ARC

It is a command by which we can create a circle segment (part of a circle) or part of the curve. An arc can be a 2-point or 3-point. In case of 3-point Arc, we can specify the angle, endpoint, start point, combination of centers, chord length, direction values and radius.

Step 1: **Ribbon:** Home tab ➢ Draw panel ➢Arc

OR

Command: A Enter,

Step 2: Specify start point of arc or [Center]: **Pick 1 point**

Step 3: Specify second point of arc or [Center/End]: **Pick 2 point**

Step 4: Specify end point of arc: **Pick 3 point**

Eleventh types of Arc:-

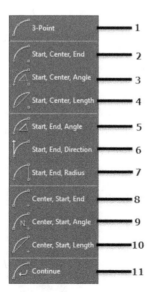

1. 3-point

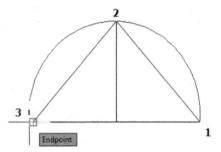

2. Start, Center, End

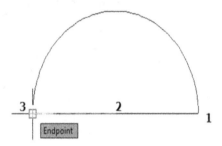

3. Start, Center, Angle

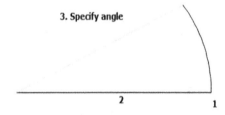

4. Start, Center, Length

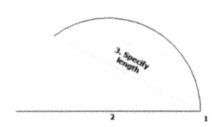

5. **Start, End, Angle**

6. **Start, End, Direction**

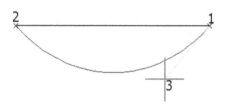

7. **Start, End, Radius**

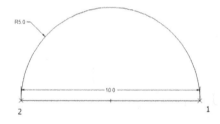

8. **Center, Start, End**

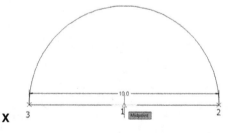

9. **Center, Start, Angle**

10. Start, Center, Length

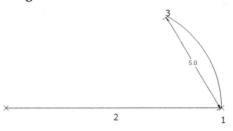

11. Continue

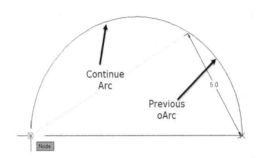

What do you mean by RECTANGLE

It is a command by which we can make a rectangle having similar right angles and two sides are also similar.

Step 1: Ribbon: Home tab ➤Draw panel➤Rectangle

OR

Command: REC Enter,

Step 2: Specify first corner point or [Chamfer/ Elevation/ Fillet/ Thickness/ Width]: **Pick 1 point**

Step 3: Specify other corner point or [Area/Dimensions/Rotation]: **Pick 2 point**

If you want select any other option Like:

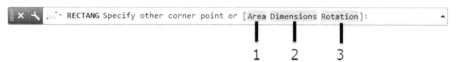

1. **Area**

   It can be explained as the region inside the boundary of any 2-d

   Step 1: Command: REC [Enter]

   Step 2: Specify first corner point or [Chamfer/ Elevation/ Fillet/ Thickness/ Width]: **Pick 1 point**

   Step 3: Specify other corner point or [Area/Dimensions/Rotation]:

   A [Enter]

   Step 4: Enter area of rectangle in current units: 500 [Enter]

   Step 5: Calculate rectangle dimensions based on [Length/Width]: L [Enter]

   Step 6: Enter rectangle length: **50** [Enter]

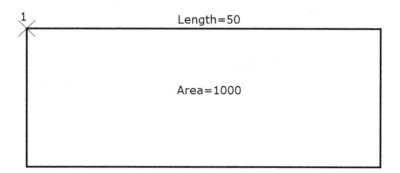

2. **Dimensions**

   Creates a rectangle by using length and width values.

   Step 1: Command: REC [Enter]

   Step 2: Specify first corner point or [Chamfer/ Elevation/ Fillet/ Thickness/ Width]: **Pick 1 point**

   Step 3: Specify other corner point or [Area/Dimensions/Rotation]: D [Enter]

Step 4: Specify length for rectangles: **50** Enter,

Step 5: Specify width for rectangles: **10** Enter,

Step 6: Specify other corner point or [Area/Dimensions/Rotation]: **Pick 2 point**

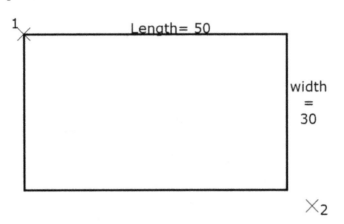

3. **Rotation**

Creates a rectangle at a specified rotation angle.

Step 1: Command: REC Enter,

Step 2: Specify other corner point or [Area/Dimensions/Rotation]: **R** Enter,

Step 3: Specify rotation angle or [Pick point]: **45** Enter,

Step 4: Specify other corner point or [Area/Dimensions/Rotation]: **D** Enter,

Step 5: Specify length for rectangles: **50** Enter,

Step 6: Specify width for rectangles: **10** Enter,

Step 7: Specify other corner point or [Area/Dimensions/Rotation]: **Pick 2 point**

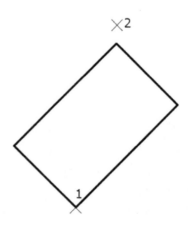

What do you mean by POLYGON

It is a command by which we can create a plane figure having at least three straight sides and angles. Triangle, rectangle and pentagon can be created through this command. In AutoCAD we can construct a polygon object that has a minimum of three closed sides and maximum of 1024 sides. There are two type Polygon. First inscribed in the circle and second circumscribed about circle.

Step 1: **Ribbon:** Home tab➢Draw panel➢Polygon

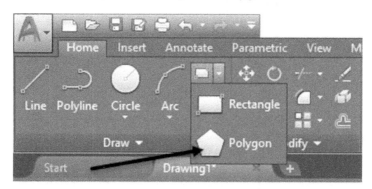

OR

Command: POL ⌷Enter.

Inscribed in the Circle

In this, the polygon lies inside the circle with its vertices on the circumference.

Step 2: Polygon enter number of sides: **8** ⌷Enter.

Step 3: Specify center of polygon or [Edge]: **Specify a canter point**

Step 4: Enter an option [Inscribed in circle/Circumscribed about circle]: **I** ⌷Enter.

Specify radius of circle: **12** ⌷Enter.

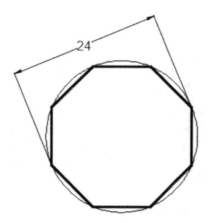

Circumscribed about Circle

It is a polygon constructed such that circles lies within it and its circumference crosses through the mid-points of the vertices of polygon.

Step 1: Command: POL

Step 2: Polygon enter number of sides: **8**

Step 3: Specify center of polygon or [Edge]: **Specify a center point**

Step 3: Enter an option [Inscribed in circle/Circumscribed about circle]: **C**

Step 4: Specify radius of circle: **10**

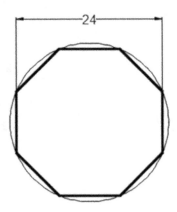

What do you mean by ELLIPSE

It is a command to create an Elliptical type arc. The first two points determine the location and length of the first axis whereas the third point fixes the distance from the center of the ellipse to the end point of the second axis.

Step 1: **Ribbon:** Home tab Draw panel Center

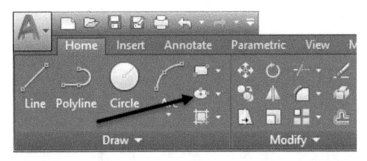

OR

Command: EL

Step 2: Specify axis endpoint of ellipse or [Arc/Center]: **Pick 1 point**

Step 3: Specify another endpoint of the axis: **10** ⏎Enter (**Give direction then enter value**)

Step 4: Specify the distance to other axis or [Rotation]: **10** ⏎Enter

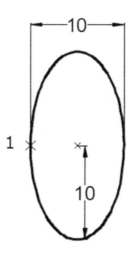

ELLIPSE Specify axis endpoint of ellipse or [Arc Center]:

1. **Arc**

   First of all. Specify first axis dimension then specify second axis dimension. Then specify start angle and end angle.

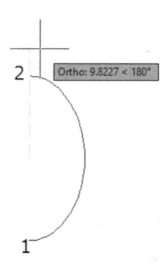

2. **Center**

Specify center point of ellipse.

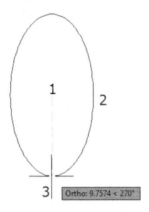

What do you mean by HATCH

It is a command to create lines for section viewing and filling of an area of an object so that it is distinguished from other objects.

Step 1: **Ribbon:** Home tab ➤Draw panel➤Hatch

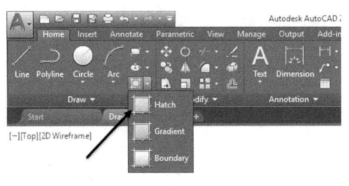

OR

Step 2: H ⏎

Step 3: Give the command 'H' enter, a ribbon toolbar will appear.

Step 4: Click "Hatch Pattern" and select the type of pattern.

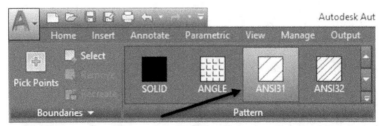

Step 5: Click on pick points and select an area that is required to be hatched. (Remember only a closed area can be hatched)

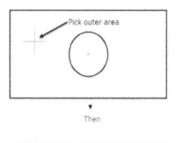

Then

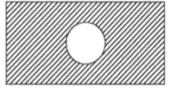

Step 6: In the ribbon toolbar, give the scale of the pattern and properties like color and background color.

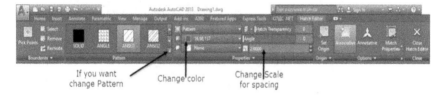

If you want change Pattern   Change color   Change Scale for spacing

Then Enter

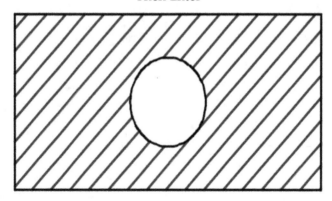

What do you mean by GRADIENT

Gradient command is used to create a gradient type of fill which means "two color types of filling." This two color types of filling is "transition filling."

Step 1: Ribbon: Home tab ➢Draw panel➢Gradient

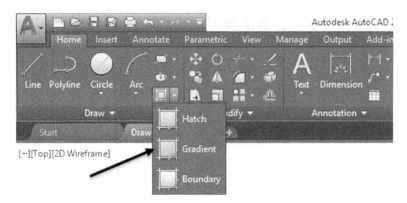

OR

Command: GD [Enter,]

Step 2: Give the command 'GD' and press enter. A ribbon toolbar will appear.

Step 3: Select the gradient pattern from 'Hatch Pattern' option.

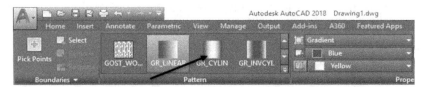

Step 4: Give the required color, such as a single or a pair of two color.

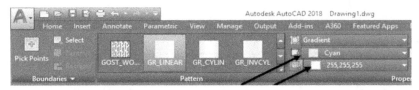

Step 5: Click 'Pick Point' to select a point in a closed area.

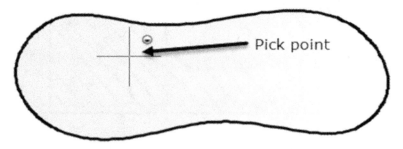

Then enter

What do you mean by BOUNDARY

Boundary command is used to create a region in an enclosed area.

Step 1: **Ribbon:** Home tab ➢Draw panel➢Boundary

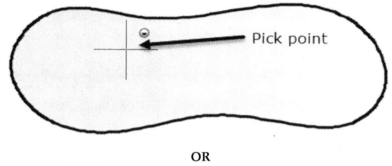

OR

Command: BO .Enter,

Step 2: On giving command 'BO' enter, a boundary creation tab appears.

Step 2: Click the option of 'pick points,' then select an enclosed point in an enclosed area that you need to make a boundary.

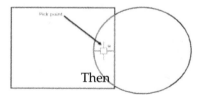

Step 3: Then enter.

What do you mean by RAY

It is a command to create a line starting from a point to infinity in one direction. It can be used as a reference for creating other objects.

Step 1: Ribbon: Home tab ➤Draw panel➤Ray

 then

OR

Command: RAY Enter

Step 2: Pick Start Point.

Step 3: Pick through point.

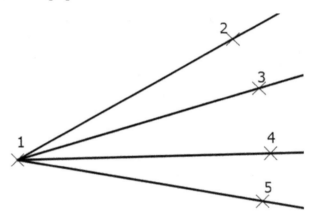

What do you mean by POINT

We used point to create point objects. With the help of this command we specify the 3d location for a point, can snap objects, view current elevation (if we neglect the z axis.)

Step 1: **Ribbon:** Home tab ➤Draw panel➤Multiple points

OR

Command: PO Enter

Step 2: Pick point.

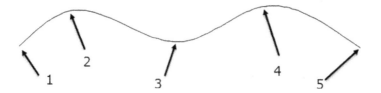

Step 3: Command: DDPTYPE [Enter] (for point style).

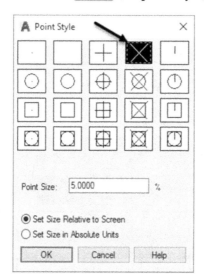

Step 3: Select point style then ok.

What do we mean by DIVIDE

When we use the command divide, it places a point along the line, arc, circle, polyline dividing it into the required number of segments.

Step 1: **Ribbon:** Home tab➢Draw panel➢Divide

Then

OR

Command: DIV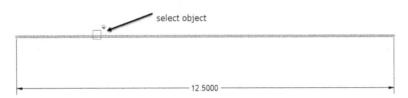

> **Step 2:** Select object to divide: **Select object**

Step 3: Enter the number of segments or [Blocks]: **5**

Step 4: **Command: PTYPE** (Select any point style and OK)

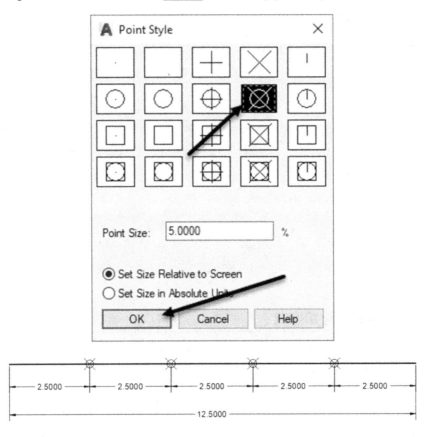

When do we use MEASURE

When we need to place points at specific required intervals along the line, polyline, arc or circle we use the command measure.

> **Step 1:** **Ribbon:** Home tab➢Draw panel➢Measure

 Then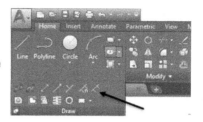

Command: ME Enter.

Step 2: Select object to measure: **Select object**

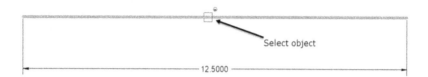

Select object

12.5000

Step 3: Specify length of segment or [Block]: **3** Enter.

Step 4: Command: PTYPE Enter. **(Select any point style and OK)**

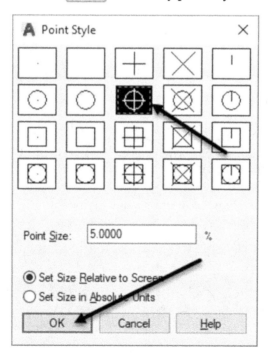

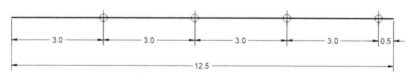

What do you mean by REGION

By using the command region, it converts a set of objects into a region object. Region is a 2D area made by different objects like arc, circle or line. It is used to convert 2d to 3d object.

    Step 1:   **Ribbon:** Home tab ➤Draw panel➤Region

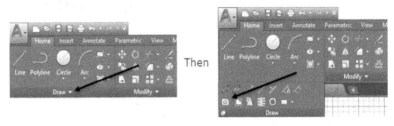

OR

Command: REG ⏎Enter,

    Step 2:   **Select object: select first object and second object then Enter**

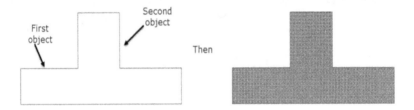

What do you mean by WIPEOUT

It is used to hideout an object whenever needed. It can be of any cross-section area made by bounded sides such as polygon, rectangle, etc. The wipe-out area can be TURN ON for editing and TURNOFF for plotting.

    Step 1:   **Ribbon:** Home tab➤Draw panel➤Wipeout

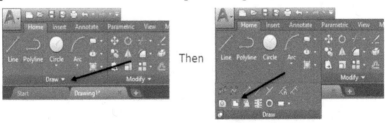

OR

Command: WIP ⏎Enter,

    Step 2:   Specify first point or [Frames/Polyline]: **Pick 1 point**

    Step 3:   Specify next point: **Pick 2 point**

    Step 4:   Specify next point or [Undo]: **Pick 3 point**

Step 5: Specify next point or [Undo/Close]: **Pick 4 point**

Step 6: Specify next point or [Undo/Close]: **C** _Enter,_

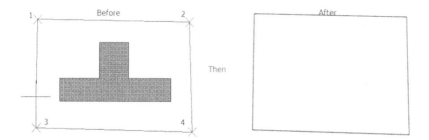

What do you mean by 3D POLYLINE

A 3D polyline is a connected sequence of straight line segments created as a single object. 3D polylines can be non-coplanar; however, they cannot include arc segments.

Step 1: **Ribbon:** Home tab➤Draw panel➤3D polyline

 Then

OR

Command: 3DPOLY _Enter,_

Step 2: Specify start point of polyline: **Pick 1 point**

Step 3: Specify end point of line or [Undo]: **Pick 2 point**

Step 4: Specify end point of line or [Undo]: **Pick 3 point**

Step 5: Specify end point of line or [Close Undo]: **Pick 4 point** _Enter,_

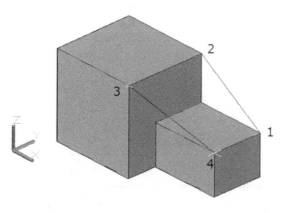

What do you mean by HELIX

Helix command creates a spring. Firstly give base radius, top radius and height as well as turns to the use of helix.

Step 1: Ribbon: Home tab➤Draw panel➤Helix

 Then

OR

Command: HELIX Enter.

Step 2: Specify center point of base: **Pick 1 point**

Step 3: Specify base radius or [Diameter]: **20** Enter.

Step 4: Specify top radius or [Diameter]: **10** Enter.

Step 4: Specify helix height or [Axis endpoint Turns Turn height tWist]: **T** Enter. **(T for turns)**

Step 4: Enter the number of turns: **10** Enter.

Step 4: Specify helix height or [Axis endpoint Turns Turn height tWist]: **15** Enter.

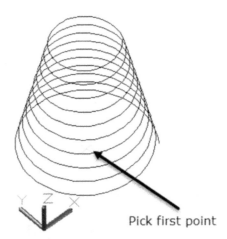

Pick first point

What do you mean by REVISION CLOUD

It is a command to highlight the area of the revision cloud. It is a series of arc formed to create a revision cloud.

Step 1: **Ribbon:** Home tab➢Draw panel➢Revision Cloud

 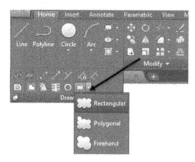

OR

Command: REVCLOUD [Enter]

Step 2: F Enter for freehand option.

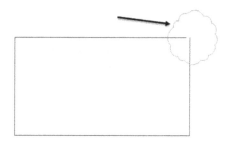

What do you mean by SOLID

It is a command to create 2d filled polygons.

Step 1: **Command: SO**

Step 2: Specify first point: **Specify a point (1)**

Step 3: Specify second point: **Specify a point (2)**

Step 4: Specify third point: **Specify a point (3)**

Step 5: Specify fourth point or <exit>: **Specify a point (1)**

Step 6: Specify third point: **Specify a point (4)**

Step 7: Specify fourth point or <exit>: **Specify a point (3)** [Enter]

What do you mean by Fill

It is used to control the filling of an object such as in the hatch, 2d solid and wide polylines. Then we need to use regenerate command to refresh the object. It is a "mode" command by which we can view the filling through on and no filling of objects through off mode.

Command: FILL ⏎ Enter

FILL enter mode [ON/OFF]: Enter option

ON

By turning the fill mode on, the complete solid object is displayed. For the filling of a 3D object to be visible, its extrusion direction must be parallel to the current viewing direction, and hidden lines must not be suppressed.

OFF

By turning the fill mode off, only the outlines of objects are displayed. Changing Fill mode affects existing objects after the drawing is regenerated. The display of line weights is not affected by the Fill mode setting.

 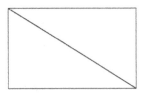

Chapter-4

Modify Tools

What do you mean by MOVE

By using move we select an object, then select its base point and move it to the required position and direction.

    Step 1:   **Ribbon:** Home tab ➤Modify panel➤Move

OR

Command: M Enter

    Step 2:   Select object Enter

    Step 3:   Specify base point or [Displacement]: Pick base point

    Step 4:   Specify second point or <use the first point as displacement>:

Give direction then 50 Enter

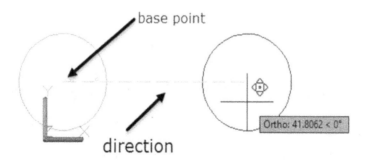

base point

direction

What do you mean by COPY

When we need the same object at more than one place, we draw an object once and then use the command 'copy' to use the same object at other places.

    Step 1:   **Ribbon:** Home tab ➤Modify panel ➤Copy

Command: CO Enter,

Step 2: Select object Enter,

Step 3: Specify base point or [Displacement/mOde]: Specify a base

Step 4: Specify second point or [Array]: **Pick first point**

Step 5: Specify second point or [Array]: **Pick second point**

Step 6: Specify second point or [Array]: **Give direction then 50** Enter,

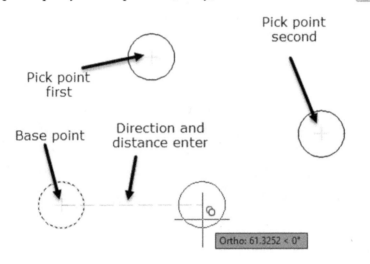

What do you mean by STRETCH

Command stretch allows us to move a portion of a drawing without distorting their connections with other parts of the drawing. But we cannot stretch Blocks, Hatch patterns, or Text entities.

Step 1: **Ribbon:** Home tab ➤Modify panel ➤Stretch

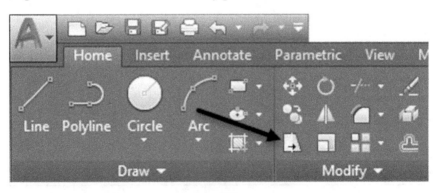

OR

Command: S Enter,

Step 2: Select object then Enter,

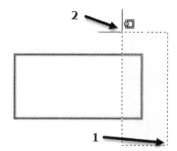

Step 3: Specify base point or [Displacement]: **Pick first point**

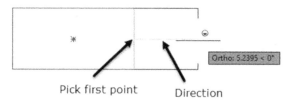

Pick first point   Direction

What do you mean by ROTATE

By using the command rotate, we can give inclination to an object from an axis.

    Step 1:   **Ribbon:** Home tab ➤Modify panel➤Rotate

OR

Command: RO .Enter.

    Step 2:   Select object then .Enter.

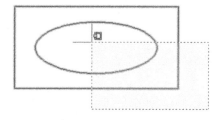

Step 2: Specify base point: Pick point

Step 3: Specify rotation angle or [Copy/Reference]: **90** Enter,

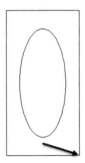

What do you mean by MIRROR

We use the mirror command to create a reflection of a designated objected about a specified axis.

Step 1: **Ribbon:** Home tab ➤Modify panel ➤Mirror

OR

Command: MI Enter,

Step 2: Select object then Enter,

Step 3: Specify first point of mirror line: **Pick first point**

Step 4: Specify second point of mirror line: **Pick second point**

Step 4: Erase source objects? [Yes/No]: **N** [Enter]

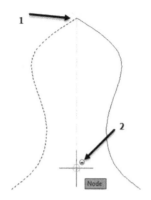

What do you mean by SCALE

By using command scale, we can alter the size of an object proportionally.

Step 1: **Ribbon:** Home tab≻ Modify panel ≻Scale

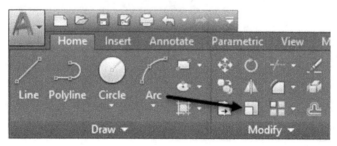

OR

Command: SC [Enter]

Step 2: **Select object then** [Enter]

Step 3: Specify base point: **Pick base point**

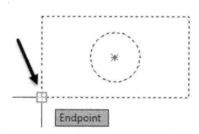

Step 4: Specify scale factor or [Copy/Reference]: R ⏎ᴱⁿᵗᵉʳ **(R enter for reference)**

Step 5: Specify reference length: **1** ⏎ᴱⁿᵗᵉʳ

Step 6: Specify new length or [Point]: **2** ⏎ᴱⁿᵗᵉʳ

Before   **After**

What do you mean by TRIM

We use command trim to erase a portion of the selected object that crosses a specified edge. In other words, we can use command trim on an object to meet edges of another object.

Step 1: **Ribbon:** Home tab ➤Modify panel➤Trim

OR

Command: TR ⏎ᴱⁿᵗᵉʳ

Step 2: Select object or <select all>: **Select reference object then** ⏎ᴱⁿᵗᵉʳ

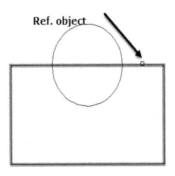

Ref. object

Step 3: Trim [Fence/Crossing/Project/eRase/Edge/Undo]: **Select trim object**

select trim object

What do you mean by EXTEND

By using the command extend, we can elongate or say lengthen a line, arc or polyline to meet a specified boundary edge.

Step 1: **Ribbon:** Home tab ➤Modify panel ➤Extend

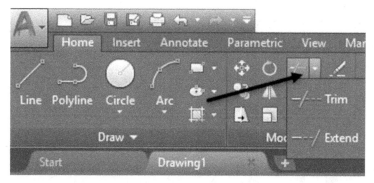

OR

Command: EX ⏎

Step 2: Select object or <select all>: **Select reference object then** ⏎

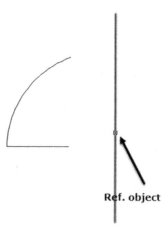

Ref. object

Step 3: Extend [Fence/Crossing/Project/Edge/Undo]: **Select Extend object**

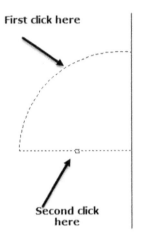

What do you mean by FILLET

We use the command fillet when need to construct an arc of specified radius between two lines, arcs, circles or vertices of polylines.

Step 1: **Ribbon:** Home tab ➤Modify panel➤Fillet

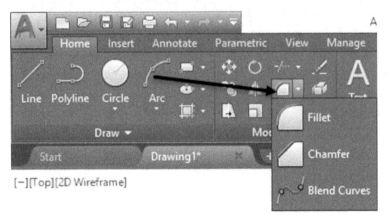

OR

Command: F Enter,

Step 2: Select first object or [Undo/Polyline/Radius/Trim/Multiple]: **R** Enter, **(R for fillet radius)**

Step 3: Specify fillet radius: **5** Enter,

Step 4: Select first object or [Undo/Polyline/Radius/Trim/Multiple]: **Select first object**

Step 5: Select second object or shift-select to apply corner or [Radius]: **Select second object**

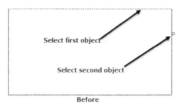

Before

After

What do you mean by CHAMFER

A chamfer is an angled line connection, by using command chamfer we create an angled connection at the intersection of two lines.

Step 1: **Ribbon:** Home tab ➢Modify panel➢Chamfer

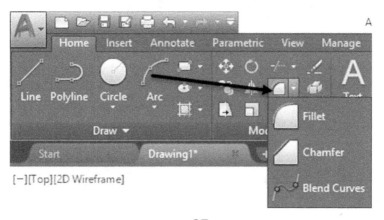

[−][Top][2D Wireframe]

OR

Command: CHA [Enter,]

Step 2: Select first line or [Undo/Polyline/Distance/Angle/Trim/mEthod/ Multiple]: **D** [Enter,] **(D enter for Distance)**

Step 3: Specify chamfer length on the first line: **5** [Enter,]

Step 4: Specify chamfer length on the first line: **10** [Enter,]

Step 5: Select first line or [Undo/Polyline/Distance/Angle/Trim/mEthod/ Multiple]: **Select first object**

Step 6: Select second line or shift select to apply corner or [Distance/Angle/ Method]: **Select second object**

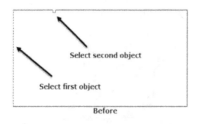

Before

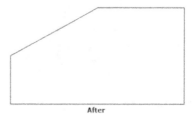

After

When do we use BLEND CURVES

When we need to join two lines or curves, we use blend curves. It creates a spline between the selected object, shape of the spline depends upon specified points while the length of the selected object remains unchanged.

Step 1: **Ribbon:** Home tab ➤Modify panel ➤Chamfer

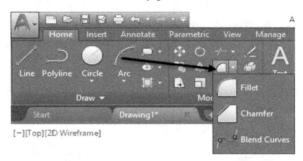

OR

Command: BLEND `Enter`

Step 2: Select first object or [CONtinuity]: **Select first object**
Step 3: Select second object: **Select second object**

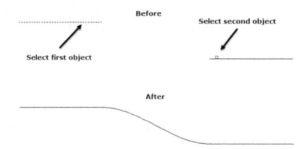

What do you mean by ARRAY

We use command array for creating a series of object in a continuous manner and the required number of rectangular, polar (circular) or any selected path.

Ribbon: Home tab ➤Modify panel ➤Array

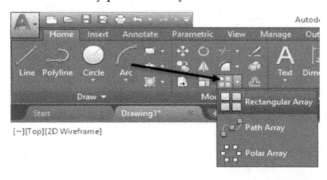

Rectangular

Rectangular Array can be copied to multiple objects. Rectangular Array object is a copy of the row and column where we can give the distance between rows and columns.

Step 1: **Command: AR** Enter,

Step 2: Select object: **Select rectangle** Enter,

Step 3: Enter array type [Rectangular/PAth/POlar]: **R** Enter,

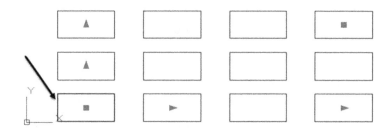

If you want to change the column distance and row distance or number

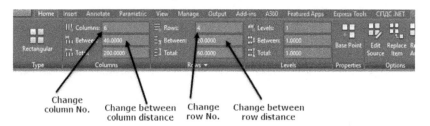

Change column No.   Change between column distance   Change row No.   Change between row distance

Then

Path

Polar Array of objects in multiple copies can be made in a circular pattern. Polor Array by the center point and the number and angle of the object copy is given to the use of Polor Array. Copy of which may be circular object.

Step 1: Command: AR ⏎Enter⏎

Step 2: Select object: **Select object** ⏎Enter⏎

Step 3: Enter array type [Rectangular/PAth/POlar]: **PA** ⏎Enter⏎

Step 4: Select curve path: **Select path**

select path

Select array
object

If you want to change the distance or number

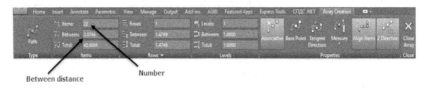

Between distance

Number

Then

Polar

Array path, the path of an object like any other object copies. The second object path which does work. The Curve is the path.

Step 1: Command: AR ⏎Enter⏎

Step 2: Select object: **Select object** ⏎Enter⏎

Step 3: Enter array type [Rectangular/PAth/POlar]: **PO** ⏎Enter⏎

Step 4: **Specify** center point of array [Base point Axis of rotation]: **Pick center point**

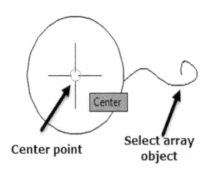

Center

Center point

Select array
object

If you want change Angle or number

Change
number

Change
angle

Then

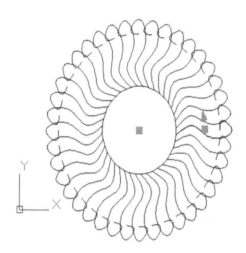

What do you mean by EXPLODE

Command Explode breaks a block, hatch pattern or dimension into its constituent entities and polyline into a series of straight lines. By using explode, we can also modify the properties of a particular object in block, etc.

Step 1: **Ribbon:** Home tab ➤Modify panel ➤Explode

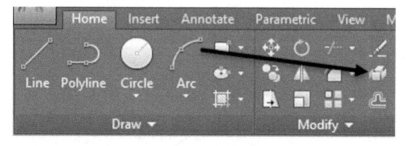

OR

Command: X [Enter]

Step 2: Select object then [Enter]

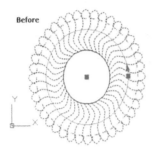
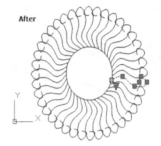

What do you mean by OFFSET

By using the command offset, we can create a new line, polyline, and arc or circle parallel to the object and at a specified distance from it.

Step 1: **Ribbon:** Home tab ➤Modify panel ➤Offset

OR

Command: O Enter

Step 2: Specify offset distance or [Through/Erase/Layer]: **1** Enter

Step 3: Select object to offset or [Exit/Undo]: **Select object**

Select object

Step 4: Specify point on side to offset or [Exit/Multiple/Undo]: **Pick a side**

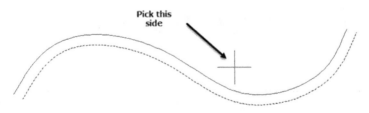

Pick this side

What do you mean by LENGTHEN

Command LENGTHEN Changes the length of an object and the included angle of arcs. We can specify changes as the final length, an increment or angle. LENGTHEN can be used as an alternative tool instead off TRIM or EXTEND.

Step 1: **Ribbon:** Home tab ➤Modify panel ➤Lengthen

Command: LEN Enter,

Step 2: Select an object to measure or [DElta Percent Total DYnamic]: **select object then P** Enter,

Step 3: Enter percentage length: **150** Enter,

What do you mean by ALIGN

We use command Align when we need to keep an object in scale with another object i.e. it usexd for aligning one or more point of an object called source point with the points of other object called definition point.

Step 1: **Ribbon:** Home tab ➤Modify➤panelAlign

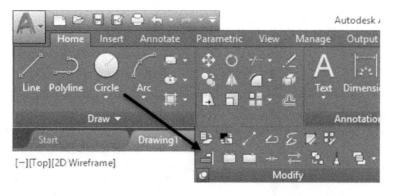

Command: AL Enter

Step 2: Select object: **Select source object**

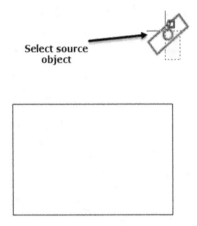

Select source
object

Step 3: Specify first source point: **Pick first point**

Step 4: Specify first destination point: **Pick second point**

Step 5: Specify second source point: **Pick third point**

Step 6: Specify second destination point: **Pick fourth point**

Step 7: Specify third destination point or <continue>: Enter

Step 8: Scale objects based on alignment point? [Yes/No]: **Y** Enter

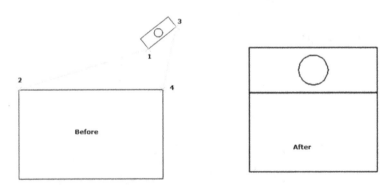

What do you mean by BREAK

By using command break, we can erase part of the line, arc or a circle or used to split it into two lines or arc. Generally, we use it for creating a gap between lines for writing text.

Step 1: **Ribbon:** Home tab ➢Modify panel ➢Break

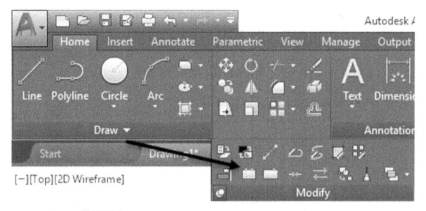

Command: BR Enter.

Step 2: **Select object**

Step 3: Specify second break point or [First point]: **F** Enter.

Step 4: Specify first break point: **Pick first point**

Step 5: Specify second break point: **Pick second point**

First point   Second point

What do you mean by JOIN?

By using Command join, we can attach two objects lying in the same plane.

Step 1: **Ribbon:** Home tab ➤Modify panel ➤Join

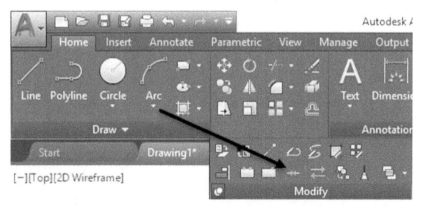

Command: J Enter.

Step 2: Select source object or multiple objects to join at once: **Select first line**

Step 3: Select objects to join: **Select second line then** Enter.

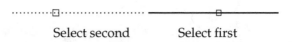

Select second   Select first

What do you mean by DELETE DUPLICATE OBJECT

This command removes duplicate or overlapping lines, arcs, and polylines. Also, combines partially overlapping or contiguous ones.

Step 1: **Ribbon:** Home tab≻Modify panel≻

Delete duplicate object

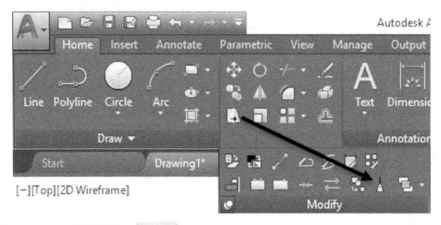

Command: OVERKILL [Enter]

Step 2: Select object then [Enter]

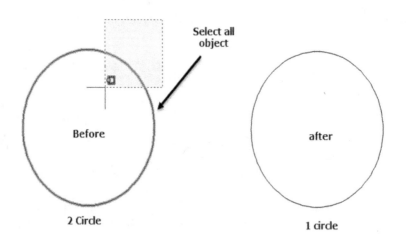

Step 3: Select all Radio Button and click Ok

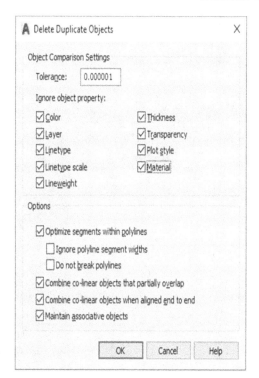

What do you mean by DRAW ORDER

Several options are available that control the order in which overlapping objects are displayed. In addition to the DRAWORDER command, the TEXTTOFRONT command brings all text, dimensions, or leaders in a drawing in front of other objects, and the HATCHTOBACK command sends all hatch objects behind other objects.

Select Objects

Specifies the objects for which you want to change the draw order. For the above and under options, an additional prompt displays in which you select the reference objects that the originally selected objects should be above or under.

Above Objects

Moves the selected object above the specified reference objects.

Under Objects

Moves the selected objects below the specified reference objects.

Front

Moves the selected objects to the top of the order of objects in the drawing.

Back

Moves the selected objects to the bottom of the order of objects in the drawing.

Step 1: **Ribbon:** Home tab≻Modify panel≻Draw order

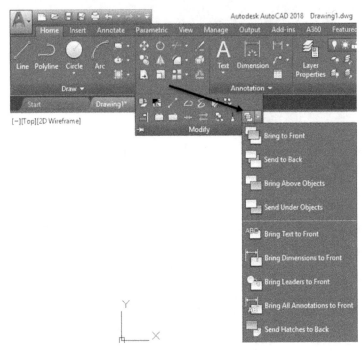

OR

Command: DR

Step 2: **Select object then** _Enter,_

Step 3: Enter object ordering option [Above objects Under objects Front Back]:
B _Enter,_

Before   After

What do you mean by BLOCKS

It is used to create a block by selecting that object and giving it an insertion point and then save it by the name of itself. These blocks are saved in the design centre toolbar and the tool palettes.

Ribbon: Insert tab ≻Block panel≻Create

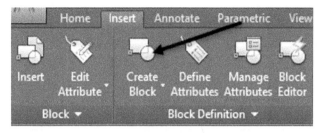

Command: B _Enter_

Step 1: Give the command 'B' and press Enter, A block definition tab appears.

Step 2: Give a name to your block followed by selecting the option of "select object" and select the object you want to convert to blocks.

Step 3: Select the base point by clicking "pick points" and give the values of X, Y and Z coordinates.

Step 4: Click OK.

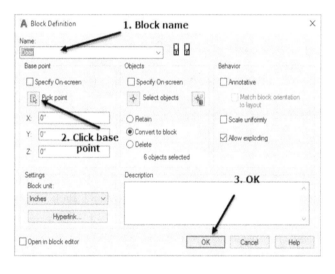

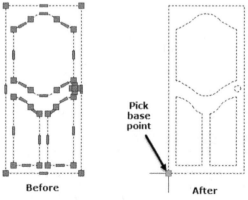

Chapter-5

Annotation

What do you mean by TEXT

It is a command to create a single-line text object. It is sometimes used to define different line text objects which we can modify, relocate.

> **Step 1:** **Ribbon:** Annotation tab ➤Text ➤Single line text

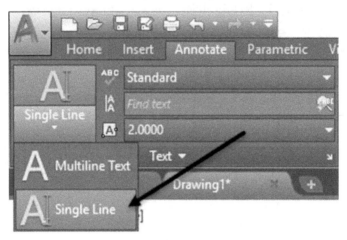

Command: DT Enter,

> **Step 2:** Specify start point of text or [Justify/Style]: **Pick Start point**
>
> **Step 3:** Specify the height: **2** Enter,
>
> **Step 4:** Specify rotation angle of the text: **30** Enter,
>
> **Step 5:** Type any text Ex: **Simranjit Singh PLM Consultant** then Enter,

What do you mean by MULTILINE TEXT

It is a used to create multiline text objects such as paragraphs. It can also be modified, relocate. Using this command, we can format text appearance, boundaries and columns.

Step 1: Ribbon: Annotation tab ➤Text ➤Multiline text

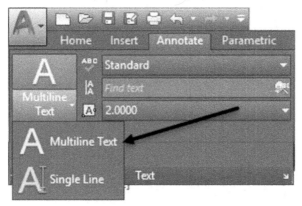

Command: MT Enter

Step 2: Specify first corner: **Pick first corner**

Step 3: Specify opposite corner or [Height/Justify/Line spacing/Rotation/Style/Width/Columns]: **Pick second corner**

Step 4: Type any text and text formatting, click Close **X**

	Name	Designation
1.	Linkan sagar	CAD Consultant
2.	Simranjit	CAD Consultant
3.	Vishal Gupta	coordinator
4.	Devesh singh	coordinator
5.	Jawed	system administrator
6.	Ritu gupta	Head counsellor
7.	Megha	counsellor
8.	Girni	counsellor
9.	Aarushi	receptionist
10.	Deep singh	Java trainer
11.	Rajeev Shishodia	Java trainer
12.	Pankaj Singh	.NET & Python
13.	Kuldeep Shishodia	Networking
14.	Vivek jha	C/C++
15.	Punit katiyar	PHP
16.	Anuj Kumar	PHP & UI
17.	Nitesh Bhardwaj	Embedded system
18.	Shashank	Digital marketing

What do you mean by TEXT STYLE

It is used to change text style like text height, text font.

Step 1: **Ribbon:** Annotation tab ➤ Text Text ➤ style

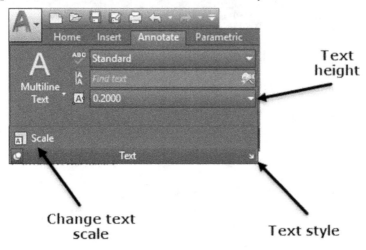

Text height

Change text scale

Text style

Text style

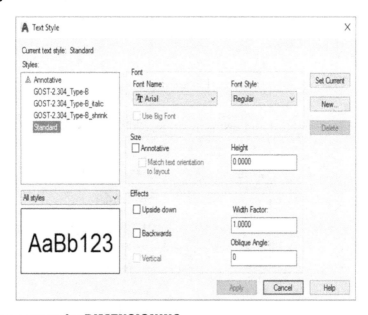

What do you mean by DIMENSIONING

It is a command with the help of which we can draw the current viewport, change current text style, undo the recently created objects, etc.

Command: DIM & DIM1 Enter

Dimensioning mode command equivalents	
Dimensioning mode Command	Equivalent Command
ALIGNED	DIMALIGNED
ANGULAR	DIMANGULAR
BASELINE	DIMBASELINE
CENTER	DIMCENTER
CONTINUE	DIMCONTINUE
DIAMETER	DIMDIAMETER
HOMETEXT	DIMEDIT Home
HORIZONTAL	DIMLINEAR Horizontal
LEADER	LEADER
JOG	DIMJOGGED
NEWTEXT	DIMEDIT New
OBLIQUE	DIMEDIT Oblique
ORDINATE	DIMORDINATE
OVERRIDE	DIMOVERRIDE
RADIUS	DIMRADIUS
RESTORE	-DIMSTYLE Restore
ROTATED	DIMLINEAR Rotated
SAVE	-DIMSTYLE Save
STATUS	-DIMSTYLE Status
TEDIT	DIMTEDIT
TROTATE	DIMEDIT Rotate
UPDATE	-DIMSTYLE Apply
VARIABLES	-DIMSTYLE Variables
VERTICAL	DIMLINEAR Vertical

What do you mean by LINEAR

We use linear command, to create a linear dimension with a vertical, horizontal, or rotated dimension line.

    Step 1:   **Ribbon:** Annotate tab➤Dimensions panel➤Linear

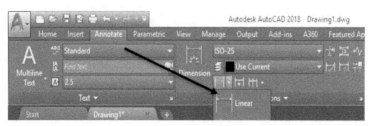

OR

Command: DIMLIN [Enter]

Step 2: Pick first point and Pick second point then give direction and click.

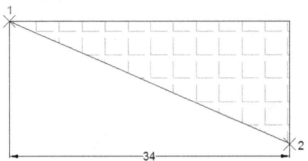

What do you mean by ALIGNED

It is a command to create a linear dimension in aligned position.

Step 1: **Ribbon:** Annotate tab➤Dimensions panel➤Aligned

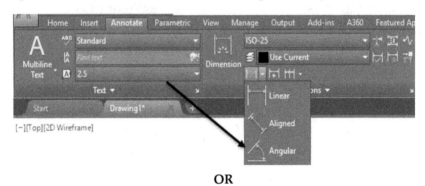

OR

Command: DIMALI

Step 2: Pick first point and Pick second point then give direction and click.

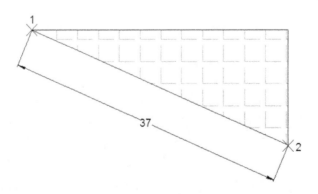

What do you mean by ANGULAR

It is a command to measure Angle of object.

Step 1: **Ribbon:** Annotate tab≻Dimensions panel≻Angular

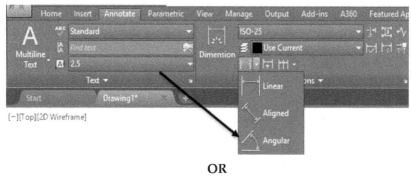

OR

Command: DIMANG ⏎

Step 2: Select first object and select second object then click.

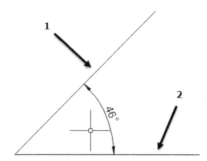

What do you mean by ARC LENGTH

It is a command to measure the length of a simple arc or polyline arc.

Step 1: **Ribbon:** Annotate tab≻Dimensions panel≻Arc length

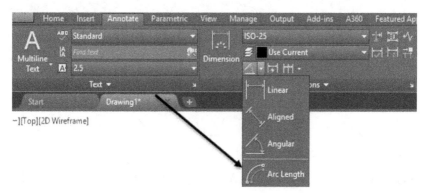

OR

Command: DIMARC `Enter`

    Step 2: Select Arc then give direction and click.

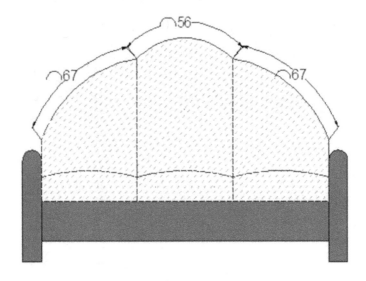

What do you mean by RADIUS

As we all know, radius is the distance between the centre point and the point on the circle or the half of the diameter. It is a command to measure the radius of a selected circle or arc and display the dimension text having a radius symbol in front of it.

    Ribbon: Annotate tab➢Dimensions panel➢Radius

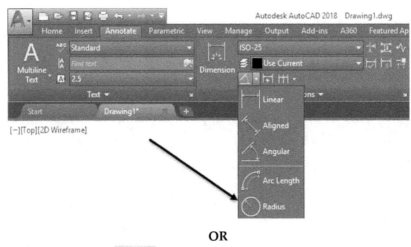

OR

Command: DIMRAD `Enter`

    Step 2: Select Circle or Arc and give direction then click.

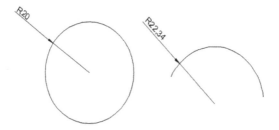

What do you mean by DIAMETER

It is a command to measure the diameter of the selected circle or arc, display the dimension text with diameter symbol in front of it and can relocate the resulting diameter dimension.

Step 1: **Ribbon:** Annotate tab ➤Dimensions panel ➤Diameter

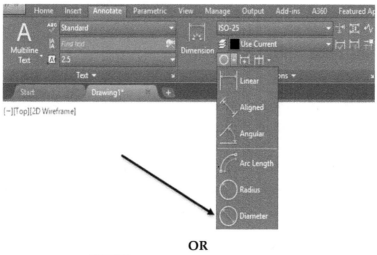

OR

Command: DIMDIA Enter,

Step 2: Select Circle or Arc and give direction then click.

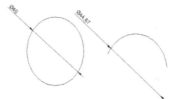

What do you mean by JOGGED RADIUS DIMENSION

It is a command that measures the radius of the selected object and displays a radius symbol with dimension text.

Step 1: **Ribbon:** Annotate tab ➤Dimensions panel ➤Jogged

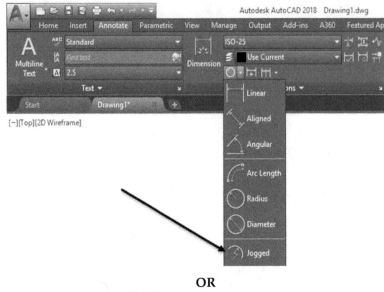

OR

Command: DIMJOGGED Enter

Step 2: Pick first arc then pick second point override center.

Step 3: Pick third point for text location then pick fourth point for direction.

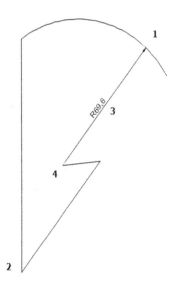

What do you mean by ORDINATE

It is a command to measure horizontal or vertical distance from the point of origin $(0, 0)$.

Step 1: **Ribbon:** Annotate tab ➢Dimensions panel ➢Ordinate

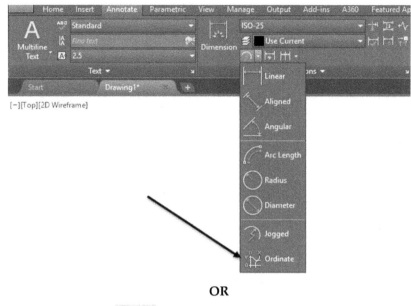

OR

Command: DIMORD Enter,

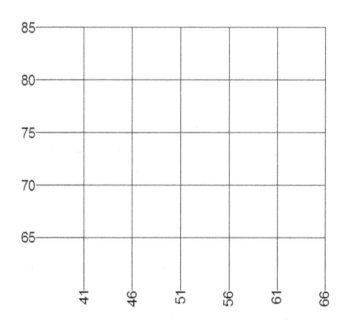

What do you mean by QUICK DIMENSION

It is a command which quickly creates multi-dimensions of the selected objects, particularly useful for dimensioning a series of circles and arcs, for creating a series of baseline.

Continuous

Creates a series of continued dimensions.

Ordinate

Creates a series of ordinate dimensions.

Staggered

Creates a series of staggered dimensions.

Radius

Creates a series of radius dimensions.

Edit

Edit a series of dimensions. When we are ready to add or remove points from existing dimensions.

Baseline

Creates a series of baseline dimensions.

Datum Point

Sets a new datum point for baseline and ordinate dimensions.

Diameter

Creates a series of diameter dimensions.

Settings

Sets the default object snap for specifying extension line origins. We get the following prompt:

Step 1: **Ribbon:** Annotate tab≻Dimensions panel≻Quick Dimension

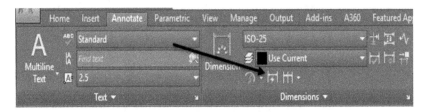

OR

Command: QDIM Enter,

Step 2: Select geometry to dimension: **Select all object then**

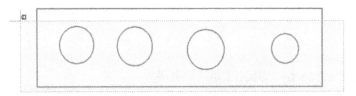

Step 3: Specify dimension line position, or [Continuous/ Staggered/ Baseline/ Ordinate/ Radius/ Diameter/ datumPoint/ Edit/ seTtings]: **Give direction and click**

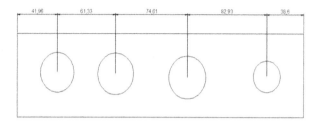

What do you mean by CONTINUE

It is a command to create an extension line automatically from the last selected linear, angular or ordinate dimension.

Step 1: **Ribbon:** Annotate tab➢Dimensions panel➢Continue

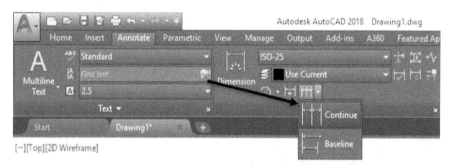

OR

Command: DIMCONT [Enter]

Step 2: Pick third point, pick fourth point and pick fifth point.

(First of all use different dimension command like aligned then use continue dimension)

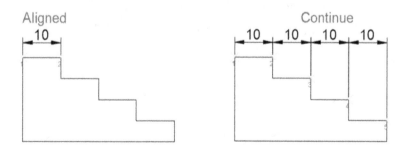

What do you mean by BASELINE

It is a command to create angular, linear and ordinate dimension from the baseline of the selected dimension.

Step 1: **Ribbon:** Annotate tab➢Dimensions panel➢Baseline

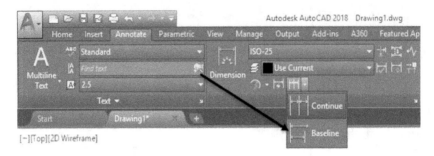

OR

Command: DIMBASE [Enter,]

Step 2: Select base dimension line and then click next point.

What do you mean by CENTRE MARK

It is a command to create a centre point in a circle or arc.

Step 1: **Ribbon:** Annotate tab ➤Centerlines ➤Center Mark

Step 2: Select arc or circle: **Select circle**

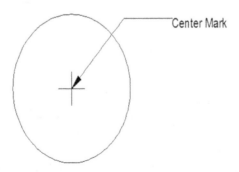

What do you mean by CENTRE LINE

It is a command to create a centerline in a line.

    Step 1:   **Ribbon:** Annotate tab ➤Centerlines ➤Center Mark

    Step 2:   Select first line then select second line.

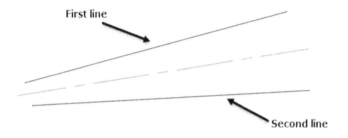

What do you mean by INSPECTION DIMENSION

It is a command to inspect the dimension given I the drawing so as to maintain the standard of the dimensions.

    Step 1:   **Ribbon:** Annotate tab ➤Dimensions panel ➤Inspect

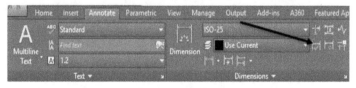

OR

Command: DIMINSPECT Enter.

    Step 2:   Select dimension then Enter. and set inspection rate.

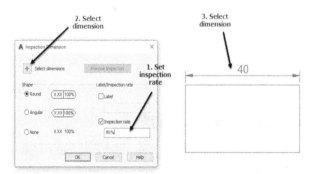

Then click OK

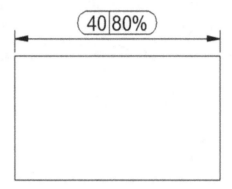

What do you mean by DIMENSION BREAK

It is a command to break or restore the dimension or extension lines when they cross each other.

Step 1: **Ribbon:** Annotate tab≻Dimensions panel ≻Break

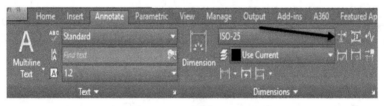

OR

Command: DIMBREAK `Enter`

Step 2: Select dimension then `Enter`

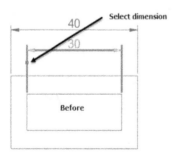

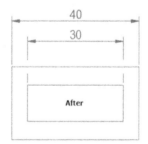

What do you mean by DIMENSION SPACE

It is a command to adjust the spacing or distance between linear or angular dimensions.

Step 1: **Ribbon:** Annotate tab ➤Dimensions panel ➤Adjust Space

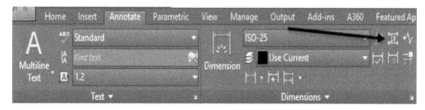

OR

Command: DIMSPACE ⏎Enter,

Step 2: Select first reference dimension and select second dimension then ⏎Enter,

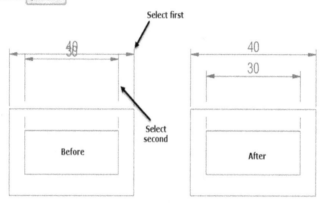

When do we use DIM STYLE

When we need to change the dimension setting and have control over the dimension used in the drawing, we use 'DIM Style". It stands for Dimension Style, by using 'dimstyle' we can create dimension styles and specify the format of dimensions quickly.

Like: Text height, Arrow size and precision etc.

Step 1: **Ribbon:** Annotate tab ➤Dimensions panel ➤Dimension Style

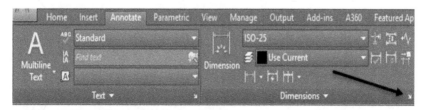

OR

Command: D ⏎Enter,

Step 2: Click modify button then select any tab like text, arrow etc.

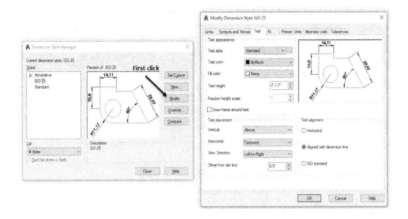

What do you mean by QLEADER

We use 'QLeader' to create leader annotation. By its help we can set location of set multiline text annotation and specify leader format

You can use QLEADER to

- Set the location where leaders attach to multiline text annotation
- Specify leader annotation and annotation format
- Constrain the angle of the first and second leader segments.
- Limit the number of leader points

Step 1: **Command: LE** Enter

Step 2: Specify first leader point, or [Settings]: **First point_**

Step 3: Specify next point: **Second point**

Step 4: Specify text width: **0**

Step 5: Enter first line of annotation text: **Wall 4.5"** Enter

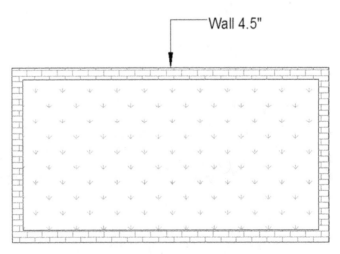

What do you mean by LEADER

It is a command to create a line that can be connected to a feature by annotation. It also draws a leader line segment to the point specified.

Step 1: Command: LEAD `Enter.`

Step 2: Specify leader start point: **Pick first point**

Step 3: Specify next point: **Pick second point**

Step 4: Specify next point or [Annotation/Format/Undo]: **Pick third point**

Step 5: Specify next point or [Annotation/Format/Undo]: **Pick fourth point**

Step 6: Specify next point or [Annotation/Format/Undo]: **A** `Enter.`

Step 7: Enter first line of annotation text or <option>: **Park** `Enter.`

Step 8: Enter next line of annotation text: `Enter.`

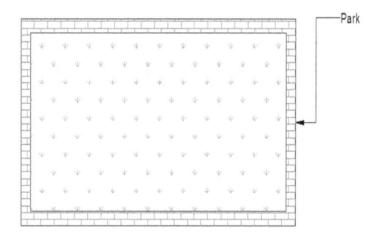

What do you mean by TABLE

It is a command to create several rows and columns in an empty table. We use table when we need to show the data input in tabular form.

Step 1: **Ribbon:** Home tab ➢Annotation panel ➢Tables

Command: TB `Enter.`

Step 1: Give the command 'TB' and press Enter.. An insert Table tab appears.

Step 2: If we have a table in excel then click the option of "from a data link" and browse the file and upload it. Else to create a new table select "Start from an empty table"

Step 3: Specify the requirements of the table in columns and rows settings.

Step 4: Click "preview" if you want a preview of your table, else click OK.

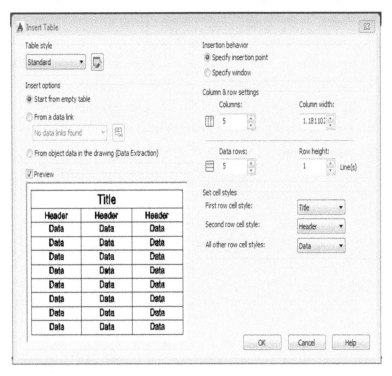

OR

Step 2: If you want link excel file so click from a data link.

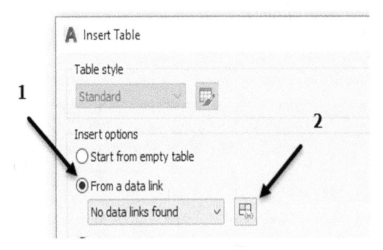

Step 3: Create a new excel data link. Then give name and press OK..

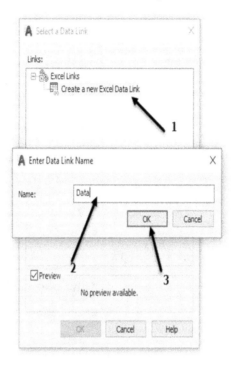

Step 4: Click browse then OK.

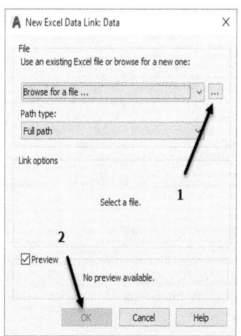

Step 5: Select Excel file then ok.

	A	B
1	**Name**	**Designation**
2	Linkan sagar	CAD Consultant
3	Simranjit	CAD Consultant
4	Anuj Kumar	PHP &UI
5	Nitish Bhardwaj	Embedded system
6	Vishal Gupta	coordinator
7	Devesh singh	coordinator
8	Mohammad Jawed Ali	system administrator
9	Ritu gupta	Head counsellor
10	Megha	counsellor
11	Ginni	counsellor
12	Aarushi	receptionist
13	Deep singh	Java trainer
14	Rajeev Shishodia	Java trainer
15	Pankaj Singh	.NET & Python
16	Kuldeep Shishodia	Networking
17	Vivek jha	C/C++
18	Punit katiyar	PHP
19	Shashank	Digital marketing

What do you mean by Smart Dimension? new

Smart Dimension tool is recently introduce in AutoCAD 2017.

This tool is use to show the dimension of an object. This tool has an existing feature by which you can check any dimension of an object. While in normal dimension tool, the dimensions of an object is different like aligned, linear, radius etc. but Smart dimension lonely work on behalf of all dimension.

Step 1: **Ribbon:** HomeAnnotate ➢Dimensions ➢Dimension.

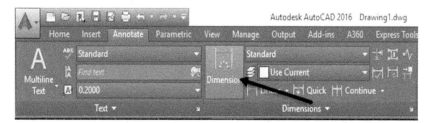

Step 2: Select object.

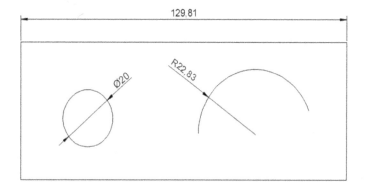

Chapter-6

Inquiry

What do you mean by LIST

When we need to know the all properties of an object, we use command LIST. It lists all information of the selected objects such as what type of object it is (whether it is a circle, arc, block etc.), what is its color, its axis, its thickness, location of its end points, elevation from z-axis.

Following information we can get through command LIST:
- Line weight, Color, line type.
- How thick the object is..?.
- Z Coordinate elevation.
- Extrusion direction (UCS coordinates), with different Z (0, 0, 1) axis.
- Information related to a particular object type such as for dimensional constraint objects, name, and value; LIST displays the constraint type, reference type (yes or no), expression.

Step 1:   **Select object then LI** Enter,

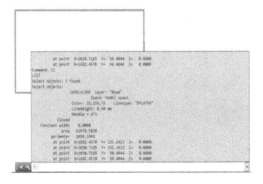

What do you mean by ANGLE

We use command ANGLE to know the angle between points, circle, or arc.
- **Step 1:**   **Ribbon:** Home tab➤Utilities panel➤Angle
- **Step 2:**   Select arc, circle, line or <Specify vertex>: **Select arc**
  Angle=130⁰

What do you mean by DIST

DIST is an inquiry command which lists the distance between any two selected points in our command bar.

Step 1: DI 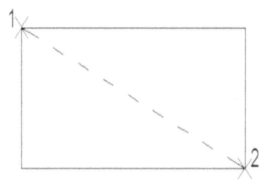 then click first point.

Step 2: Click second click.

And press F2 key

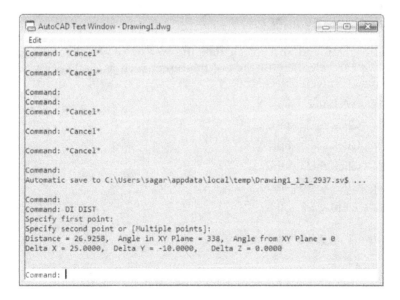

What do you mean by VOLUME

We use volume command, to compute volume of a defined object.

Step 1: **Ribbon:** Home tab➢Utilities panel➢Volume

Step 2: Click first point.

Step 3: Click second point.

Step 4: Click third point.

Step 5: Click forth point.

Step 6: T Enter for total.

Step 7: 5 Enter for height.

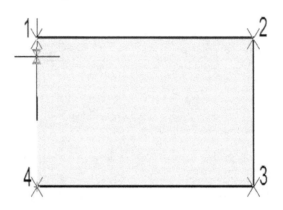

Volume=1250.00

What do you mean by AREA

We use the command area to calculate the area of an object or shape. Using this command, we can calculate the area of the object such as circle or by selecting the various points of a given object etc.

Step 1: AA Enter.

Step 2: Click first point.

Step 3: Click second point.

Step 4: Click third point.

Step 5: Click forth point.

Step 6: T Enter for total.

And press F2 key

```
AutoCAD Text Window - Drawing1.dwg                              ─   □   ✕

 Edit
Specify next point or [Arc/Length/Undo/Total] <Total>: t

Area = 250.0000, Perimeter = 70.0000
Command: Specify opposite corner or [Fence/WPolygon/CPolygon]:
Command: AREA

Specify first corner point or [Object/Add area/Subtract area] <Object>: *Canc

Command: Specify opposite corner or [Fence/WPolygon/CPolygon]:
Command: *Cancel*

Command: aa AREA
Specify first corner point or [Object/Add area/Subtract area] <Object>:
Specify next point or [Arc/Length/Undo]:
Specify next point or [Arc/Length/Undo]:
Specify next point or [Arc/Length/Undo/Total] <Total>:
Specify next point or [Arc/Length/Undo/Total] <Total>: t

Area = 250.0000, Perimeter = 70.0000

Command: |
```

Chapter-7

Parametric

What is meant by PARAMETRIC DRAWINGS

By using Parametric constraints, we can force an object to behave the way we want it to. If we need an object to behave the same way as other we need to set a constraint on it to do the same. For example, if we need a pair of line to always remain parallel to one another we can select constraint parallel, then even if we change the position of any one object the other will also change accordingly being always parallel to the first.

In the Parametric tool panels, Constraints are divided into three sections:

GEOMETRIC CONSTRAINTS
DIMENSIONAL CONSTRAINTS
MANAGE

Ribbon: Parametric

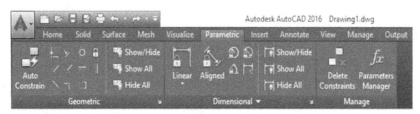

Menu: Parametric

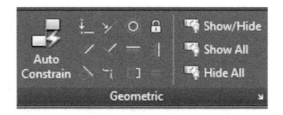

Geometric Constraints: Constrains a object based on geometric properties : Vertical, horizontal, etc

Dimensional Constraints an object based on a set length or radius

GEOMETRIC CONSTRAINTS

Ribbon: Parametric ➤Geometric

Menu: Parametric ➤Constraints

Geometric constraints associate geometric objects together. For example, If we have a symmetric drawing and later we make a change in the drawing, now the work will no longer remain symmetric, to maintain symmetricity of the drawing we apply the constraints symmetry and select the objects that we require to keep symmetrical.

Let's say we have a rectangle. As for rectangle, sides have to be perpendicular to each other. But in case during the design, we may need to change the position of a vertex. If we extend one of the rectangle vertex, then it would not remain a rectangle anymore. As AutoCAD is not aware that we want to keep it as a rectangle.

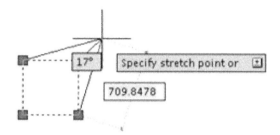

To prevent this, in AutoCAD, we apply perpendicular constraints, ensuring that we want them always perpendicular to each other. So now we add a perpendicular constraint to the two sides. Now, try to stretch the vertex again.

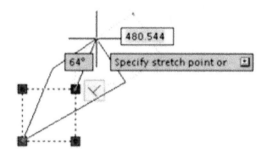

As we can see, the two sides are perpendicular to each other. But the other edges don't. So, we need to add all constraint to keep it a rectangle.

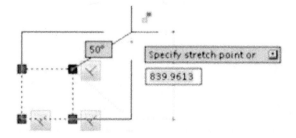

Geometric tool	Before	After

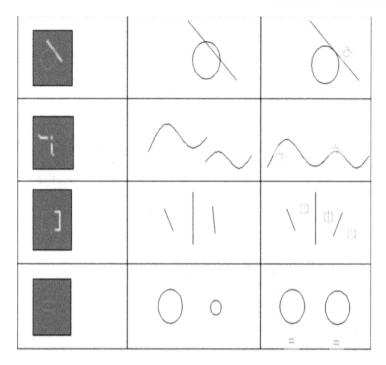

DIMENSIONAL CONSTRAINTS

Dimensional constraints are different to geometrical; these are used in making changes to what we have already worked with. If we have a drawing and we need to make amendments in the dimensions of the objects we use dimensional constraints

Instead of making a line vertical (for example), we can make a line 10 units long and make it stay that way until we change it. We can add more than one dimensional constraint on certain objects.

Draw a random angled line on the screen. Pick on the Aligned constraint icon. ^{Aligned} Pick two points on the line.

Notice that even if we have our Osnaps off, we can only pick the endpoints and midpoint on the line. After selecting the 2 points, we can now enter a length that we want the distance between those points to be.

With the constraint still highlighted, enter a number. D3 in this example refers to the 3rd dimensional constraint in the drawing. If we add a constraint from end to middle, add another from end to end (or vice versa). Notice that the constraint will be double the first one. If we change one, the other will change accordingly.

How to MANAGE CONSTRAINTS

In the third column of parametric toolbar we have 'manage' section. In this section we can perform two operations, we can use "parameters manager" to generate excel sheets of all the constraints used and secondly "delete constraints" to remove unnecessary constraints. By using Parameter manager, the excel sheet of parameter is generated, using this sheet we can also make changes in the sheet that are simultaneously applied on the objects in the drawing.

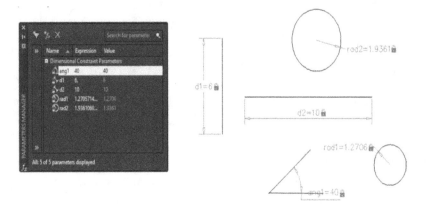

Chapter-8

Setting & Option

What do you mean by INFER CONSTRAINT

It a helping type of tool for applying geometrical constraints while creating and editing geometrical objects. We can also use it as parametric constraint and also creates line infer on and off.

INFER CONSTRAINT command automatically applies constraints between the object or points associated with object snaps and the object we are creating or editing.

Similarly AUTOCONSTRAIN command, constraints are applied only if the objects meet the constraint conditions.

With Infer Constraints turned on, to infer geometric constraint we specify the object snap while creating geometry. However, the following object snaps are not supported: Apparent Intersection, and Quadrant, Extension, Intersection

The following constraints cannot be implied:

- Smooth
- Symmetric
- Equal
- Concentric
- Fix
- Collinear

Toolbar: Status bar ➤Infer

Create a line infer off and create a line infer on.

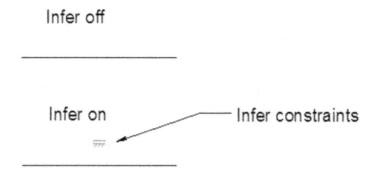

Right click for Infer setting

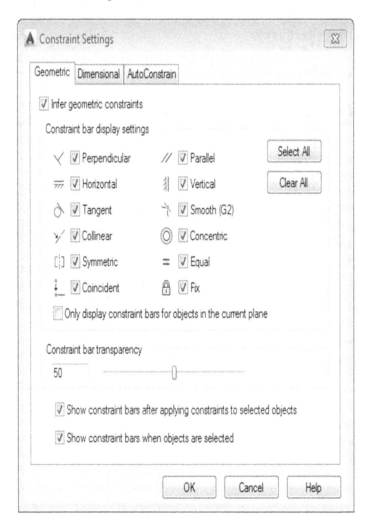

What do you mean by GRID & SNAP

The grid is a pattern of straight lines that crosses over each other, forming square. In AutoCAD it is infinite in the given workspace. Grid helps us in aligning objects and visualizing the distances between them. Horizontal lines are said to be minor grid lines and vertical lines are said to be major grid lines.

Snap mode limits the movement of the crosshairs since it is defined. With Snap mode on, the cursor will follow an invisible rectangular grid. Snap is helpful in specifying precise points with the arrow keys.

Both are independent to each other but sometimes we use them simultaneously.

Toolbar: Status bar ➤ Grid or Snap

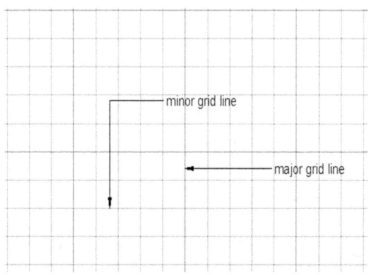

What do you mean by OSNAP

"OSNAP" means object snap. The Object Snaps are drawing tool that help us in drawing accurately. Osnap specifies us to *snap* onto a particular point location while picking a point. For example, using Osnap we can sharply pick the end point of a line or the center of a circle. Osnap in AutoCAD is so essential that we cannot draw faultlessly without them.

Toolbar: Status bar ➢Osnap

ENDPOINT: The Endpoint command snaps to the end points of arcs, line and to polyline vertices.

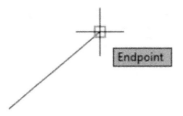

MIDPOINT: The Midpoint command snaps to the mid-point of lines and arcs and to the mid-point of polyline segments.

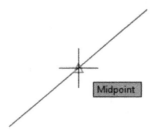

INTERSECTION: The Intersection command snaps to the physical intersection of any two drawing sheet.

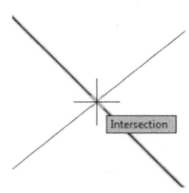

APPARENT INTERSECT: Apparent Intersection command snaps to the point where objects seems to intersect in the current view.

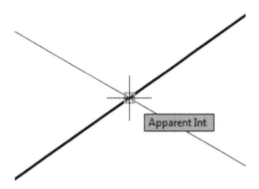

EXTENSION: The Extension command helps to snap to some point along the imaginary extension of the arc, the line, or polyline segment.

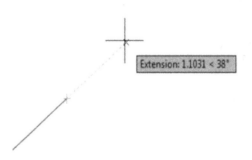

CENTRE: The Centre command snaps to the center of a circle, arc, an object or polyline arc segment.

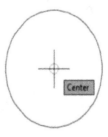

QUADRANT: The Quadrant command locates the four circle quadrant points located at east, north, west and south or 0, 90, 180 and 270 degrees respectively.

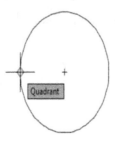

TANGENT: The Tangent command snaps to a tangent point on a circle.

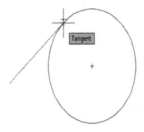

PERPENDICULAR: The Perpendicular command snaps to a point where it forms a perpendicular line with the selected object.

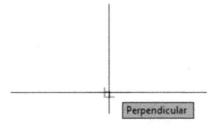

PARALLEL: The parallel command is used to draw a line parallel to a line segment.

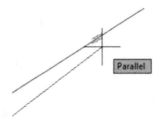

INSERT: The Insert command snaps to the insertion point of the text, block or image.

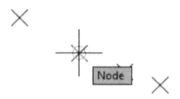

NODE: The Node command snaps to the centre of a Point object.

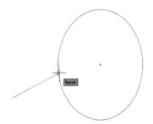

NEAREST: The nearest command snaps the nearest point on the drawing sheet.

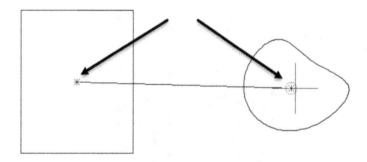

Geometric Center: Snaps to the Geometric center point of polyline, 2D polyline and 2D spline.

What do you mean by POLAR

It is a helping type of tool used to define an angle and to draw using angles. It setting contains two types of angles:

- INCREMENT ANGLE
- ADDITIONAL ANGLE

Increment angle is the angle that is shown in the drawing as a multiple of it, but additional angle we take more than one and they can be easily seen in the drawing.

Toolbar: Status bar ➤Polor

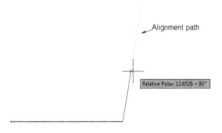

What do you mean by ORTHO

It is a setting by which cursor movement is constrained to vertical and horizontal direction only. We use it often when we specify the distance and angle between two points.

Toolbar: Status bar ➤Ortho

Ortho off   Ortho on

What do you mean by OTRACK

It is a command that hover over the reference point until the Otrack box appears. Otrack point can be changed whenever needed.

Toolbar: Status bar ➤Otrack

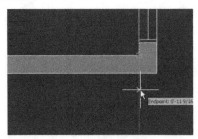

What do you mean by LWT

It is a command used to increase and decrease the pixels of the line segment.
Toolbar: Status bar➤**Lwt**

LWT OFF   LWT ON

What do you mean by DYN

It is a setting in the status bar which acts as a command interface near the cursor so as to keep the focus in the drafting area.
Toolbar: Status bar➤**Dyn**

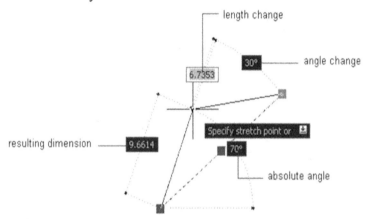

What do you mean by QP (Quick properties)

It is used to observe the properties of the required object such as color, layer, linetype, centre x, centre y, circumference, area, diameter, radius.
Toolbar: Status bar ➤QP

Select object then modify properties like radius, color etc.

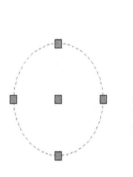 

What do you mean by COLOUR

It is a display type of tool which is used in interface elements so that the elements used can be distinguished from one another.

Command: OP Enter.

1 **Click display tab**

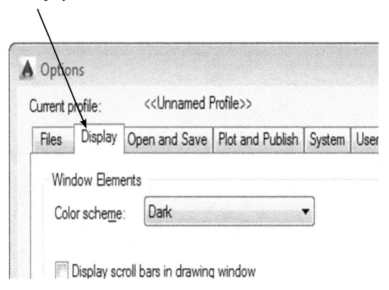

2 **Click Colors**

3 **Chose interface element & color**

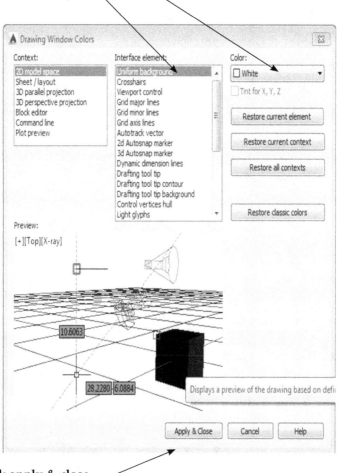

4 **Click apply & close**
5 **Click apply & ok**

What do you mean by UI COLOUR CHANGES

It is the latest setting in the AUTOCAD 2018 used to change the color to light and dark version so as to be identified easily in dark. It decreases the contrast between the elements used (tools) and workspace. It also helps in Lessing the strain on the user.

Command: OP [Enter]

1   **Click display & Chose color scheme.**

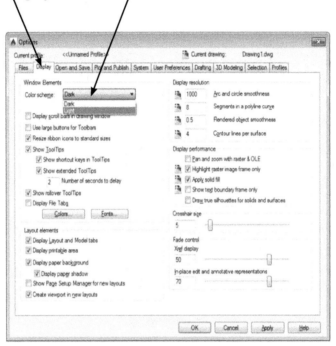

Dark

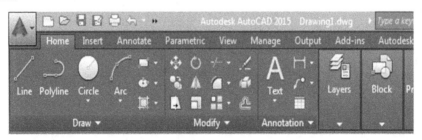

Light

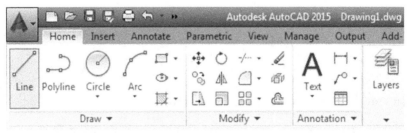

What do you mean by PAN

It is a command to move view planar to the home screen.

Menu: View ➤Zoom➤Pan

Command: P ⏎Enter⏎

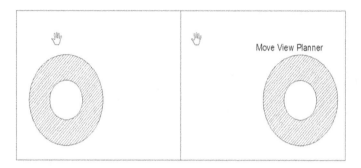

What do you mean by STEERING WHEELS

It is a navigation wheel to have a watch on the drawing made in 2-d or 3-d. some of the tools in the navigation wheel are:

- **ZOOM:** *To show a smaller area of an image at higher magnification or a larger area at a lower magnification.*
- **REWIND:** It restores the most recent view. By clicking and dragging left or right, we can move backward or forward respectively.
- **PAN:** By panning we can reposition the current view.
- **ORBIT:** Rotates the current view around a fixed pivot point.
- **WALK:** Pretend walking through a model.
- **CENTRE:** To adjust the center of the current view by specifying a point on a model or change the target point used for some of the navigation tools.
- **UP/DOWN:** Slides the current view of a model along the Z axis of the model.

LOOK: Turns around the current view.

Command: WHEEL

What do you mean by GRIPS EDITING

It is an editing option for the grip in the line. In editing the grip, we can change the size and color of the grip.

Command: GR

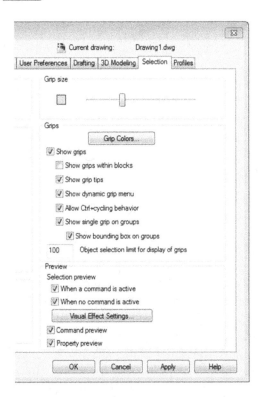

What do you mean by REGEN

It is a command to regenerate the entire drawing in the current viewport.

Menu: View ➤Regen

Command: RE Enter

Before Regen   After Regen

What do you mean by MULTLINE STYLE

It is a command to set the elements and the properties of the new multiline style or it can change them for the existing multiline style.

Menu: Format➤Multiline Style

Command: MLSTYLE

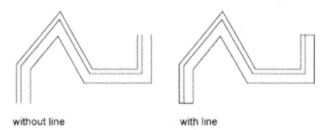

without line   with line

What do you mean by POINTSTYLE

It is a command that shows and can change the current point style and size of the point style.

Menu: Format ➤Point Style

Command: PTYPE Enter

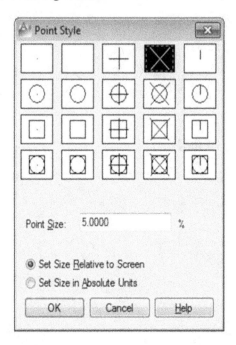

What do you mean by TABLESTYLE

The overall look of the table is denoted by table style. We can use the default table style, STANDARD, or create own table styles.

When we create a new table style, we can specify a starting table. Once the table is selected, you can specify the structure and contents to copy from that table to the table style.

Ribbon: Annotate tab ➤Tables panel ➤Tables style

Menu: Format ➤Tables style

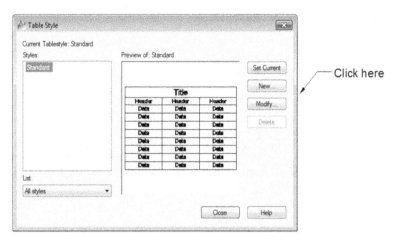

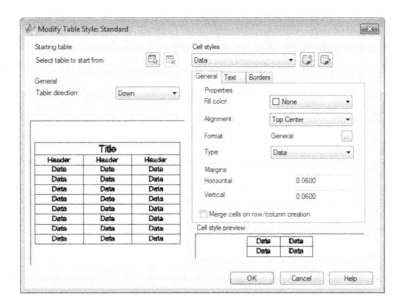

What do you mean by BACKGROUND MASK

It is a command which is used for mtext for applying background mask. In background mask dialogue box, we can specify border offset and can fill color. It can also be applied in dimension objects.

Right click and click Background Mask.

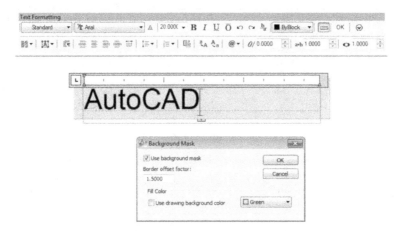

When do we use UNITS

When we begin our new work we start by setting up the units of measurement in which we need to work. When we give the command for unit, we see the Drawing Units dialogue box. The dialogue box is divided into four main sections, namely

'Length,' 'Angle,' 'Insertion Scale.' In "Length" we select our linear units whereas in "Angles," we select our angular units. We can make amendments for linear units and angular units independently and in both sections we can also control the type and precision required. In the Angle section we can also specify the direction of angle as per our requirement and ease.

LINEAR UNITS

The default unit for length is "Decimal." The AutoCAD 2018 provides five different linear unit types in its box. Brief necessary description of the different units is provided in the table below.

Unit Type	1.5 Drawing Units	1500 Drawing Units	Description
Decimal	1.5000	1500.0000	Metric or SI units
Scientific	1.5000E+00	1.5000E+03	Decimal value raised to a power
Engineering	0'-1.5000"	125'-0.0000"	Feet and decimal inches
Architectural	0'-1 1/2"	125'-0"	Feet and fractional inches
Fractional	1 ½	1500	Whole numbers and fractions

ANGULAR UNITS

As linear, the default angular unit is also decimal and in general circumstances it is not required to be changed. We will find five different angular units provided to us in the units dialogue box. Below is a table describing the necessary description of the types of angular units?

Unit Type	12.5 Angular Units	180 Angular Units	Description
Decimal Degrees	12.500	180.000	Metric units
Deg/Min/Sec	12d30'0"	180d0'0"	Degrees, Minutes and Seconds
Grads	13.889g	200.000g	400 grads = 360 degrees
Radians	0.218r	3.142r	2 Pi radians = 360 degrees
Surveyor	N 77d30'0" E	W	Compass bearings

What do you mean by LAYERS

It is a command having large space where all types of object are placed, and the basic designing is done on it…

On starting AutoCAD default layer is only shown which is set current. The person using it defines the various different layers .the object defined is only seen on the layer, the layer itself is not seen. Layer is invisible matter…..

Ribbon: Home tab ≻Layers panel ≻Layer Properties Manager

Menu: Format ≻Layer

Command: LA ↵Enter,

1. **Choose:** Format, Layer.

     Or

2. **Type:** LAYER at the command prompt.

    Command: **LAYER (or LA)**

     Or

3. **Pick:** the layers icon from the Layer Control box on the object properties toolbar.

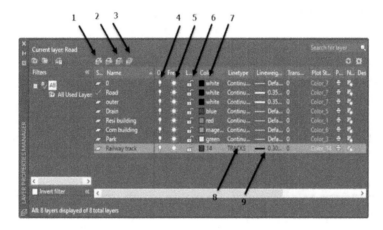

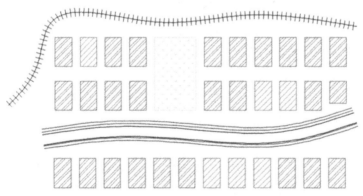

New	Creates new layers.
?	Lists layers, with states, colors and linetypes.
Make	Creates a new layer and makes it current.
Set	Sets current layer.
ON	Turns on specified layers.
OFF	Turns off specified layers.
Color	Assigns color to specified layers.

Ltype	Assigns linetype to specified layers.
Freeze	Completely ignores layers during regeneration.
Thaw	Unfreezes specified layers Ltype.
Lock	Makes a layer read only preventing entities from being Edited but available visual reference and osnap functions.
Unlock	Places a layer in read write mode and available for edits.
Plot	Turns a Layer On for Plotting
No Plot	Turns a Layer Off for Plotting
LWeight	Controls the line weight for each layer

TIP:

Layers can be set using the command line prompts for layers. To use this,

Type –LAYER or -LA at the command prompt

1. **Type** Command: **-LAYER** or **LA**
2. **Type** One of the following layer options ?/Make/Set/New/ON/OFF/ Color/Ltype/Freeze/Thaw:

Changing the Layer of an Object

1. **Click** Once on the object to change.
2. **Select** the desired layer from the Layer Control Box, AutoCAD will move the object to the new layer.

What do you mean by PURGE

Purge is basically a command for removing unused named items from a drawing... It can remove block definition, layers, dimension style, linetypes, empty text objects and text style.

Menu: Application menu ➤Drawing Utilites ➤Purge

Command: PU Enter,

Chapter-9

3D Modeling & View

BOX

Box is a 3D object. It can be create on X and Y plane and its height create on Z axis. Solid box create by this command.

Step 1: RibbonHome tabModelingBox

Step 2: Click first point for first corner.

Step 3: L Enter for box length.

Step 4: 60 Enter for length.

Step 5: 30 Enter for width.

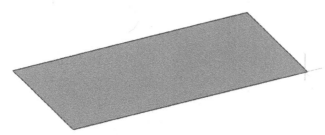

Step 6: 30 Enter for height.

CYLINDER

Cylinder command is like a circular pipe. To create cylinder we must have radius and height. After creating cylinder on x and y plane give height on z axis.

Step 1: Ribbon ➤Home tab➤Modeling➤Cylinder.

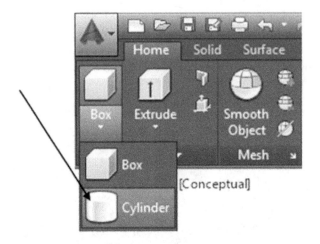

Step 2: Click point for center point.

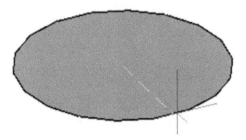

Step 3: 20 Enter for base radius.

Step 4: 30 Enter for height.

HELIX

Helix command creates a spring. Firstly give base radius, top radius and height as well as turns to the use of helix.

Step 1: Ribbon ➤Home tab ➤Draw ➤Helix.

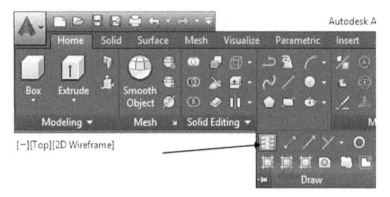

Step 2: Click point for center base point.

Step 3: 20 Enter for base radius.

Step 4: 30 Enter for top radius.

Step 5: T Enter for helix turns.

Step 6: 10 Enter for turns.

Step 7: 50 Enter for height.

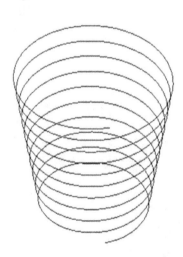

CONE

Cone command is used to create circular cone. To create cone firstly give radius after that give height of cone.

Step 1: Ribbon ➤Home tab ➤Modeling ➤Cone.

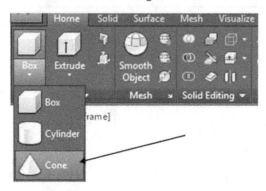

Step 2: Click point for center point.

Step 3: 20 Enter for cone radius.

Step 4: 40 Enter for cone height.

TORUS

Torus command is used to create tube and give radius of circular tube and then give radius its thickness.

Step 1: Ribbon ➤Home tab ➤Modeling ➤Torus.

Step 2:   Click point for center point.

Step 3:   20 Enter for torus radius.

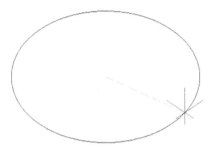

Step 4:   5 Enter for tube radius.

PYRAMID

Pyramid command is just like cone, but cone is circular while pyramid have edge, it has at least 3 edge and can up to maximum 32.

Step 1:   RibbonHome tab ➢Modeling ➢Pyramid.

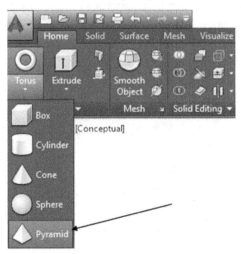

Step 2: Click point for center point.

Step 3: 10 Enter for base radius.

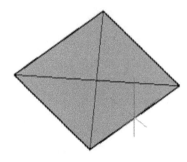

Step 4: 20 Enter for height.

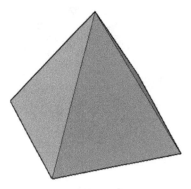

WEDGE

Sphere command act like a ball, and create just like circle. But circle is 2d object while sphere is a circular shape solid 3d object, and created by giving center and radius.

Step 1 Ribbon ➤Home tab ➤Modeling ➤Wedge.

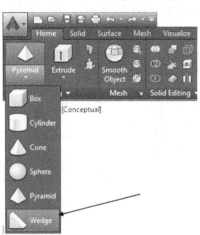

Step 2: Click first point for wedge corner.

Step 3: L Enter for length option.

Step 4: 40 Enter for length.

Step 5: 20 Enter for width.

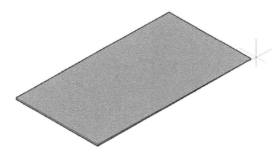

Step 6: 15 Enter for height.

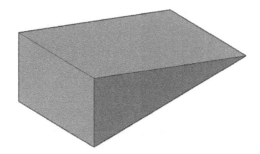

POLYSOLID

Polysolid command use just like Polyline, but polysolid is a 3d object so we also consider or give thickness and height.

It used to create wall or simple plane (surface).

Step 1: Ribbon ➤Home tab ➤Modeling ➤Polysolid.

[−][SW Isometric][Conceptual]

Step 2: H Enter for height option.

Step 3: 10' Enter for height.

Step 4: W Enter for width option.

Step 5: 9" Enter for width.

Step 6: Click first point.

Step 7: Specify direction then 60' Enter.

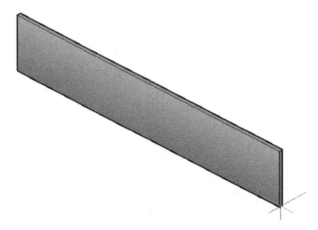

Step 8: Specify direction then 30' Enter.

Step 9: Specify direction then 60' Enter.

Step 10: C Enter for close.

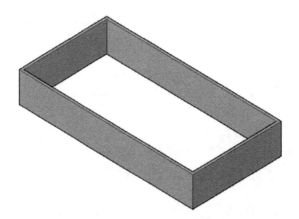

SPHERE

Sphere command act like a ball, and create just like circle. But circle is 2d object while sphere is a circular shape solid 3d object, and created by giving center and radius.

Step 1: Ribbon ➤Home tab ➤Modeling ➤Sphere.

Step 2: Click point for center point.

Step 3: 20 Enter for radius.

EXTRUDE

Extrude command is used to increase the height of object like line, circle, rectangle, arc, spline etc.

That is by increasing height we convert those 2D object into 3D.

For example. If you take a circle and extend the height you can convert it in to cylinder (3D object) or convert a rectangle into box (I.e. 3D object)

Step 1: Ribbon ➢Home tab ➢Modeling ➢Extrude.

Step 2: Select 2D object then Enter.

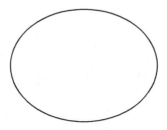

Step 3: 30 Enter for extrude height.

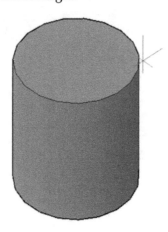

PRESSPULL

Presspull act like extrude command with a significancial difference, it allow to increase or decrease any face of the 3d object while extrude allow only increase in height of 2d.

Step 1: Ribbon ≻Home tab ≻Modeling ≻Presspull.

Step 2: Select face for presspull.

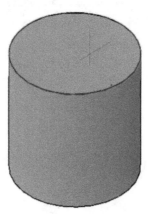

Step 3: 10 Enter for extrusion height.

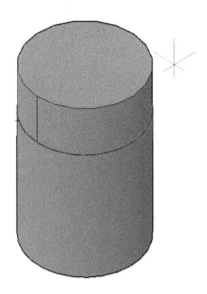

LOFT

Loft command is used to convert two or more than two 2d object into single 3d object. Loft command work on any 2d object which is built upon

Any 3rd object by selecting simultaneously both the object and then convert in single 3d object.

To use this command both object have different Z-axis (i.e. height must be different).

Step 1: Ribbon ➤Home tab ➤Modeling ➤Loft.

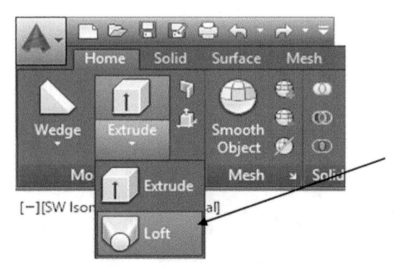

Step 2:   Select first object.

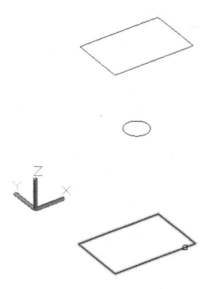

Step 3:   Select second object.

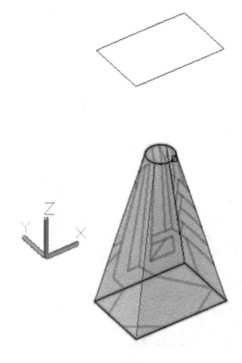

Step 4: Select third object.

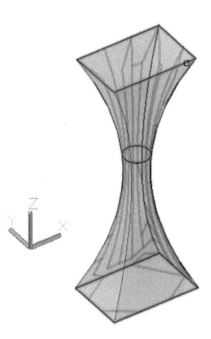

Step 5: Double enter.

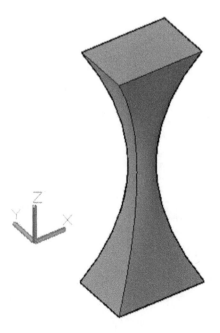

REVOLVE

Revolve command is use to convert a 2d object into 3d by revolving that object on one of any axis with respect to 2 distinguish point of that axes.

That is choose two different point on that targeted axis and revolve the object circle with respect to that point.

Step 1:   Ribbon ➤Home tab ➤Modeling ➤Revolve.

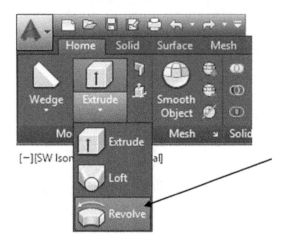

Step 2:   Select 2D object then Enter.

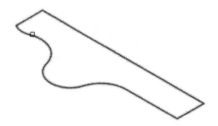

Step 3:   Click first point for Axis.

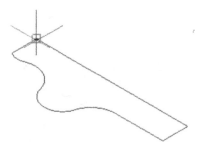

Step 4:   Click second point for Axis.

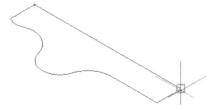

Step 5:   360 Enter for Circular angle.

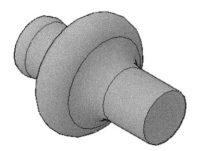

SWEEP

Sweep command is used to convert into 3d object by sweeping anyone 2d object to another 2d object.

Step 1:   Ribbon ➤Home tab ➤Modeling ➤Sweep.

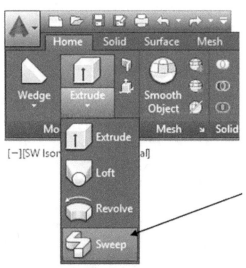

Step 2: Select object to sweep then Enter.

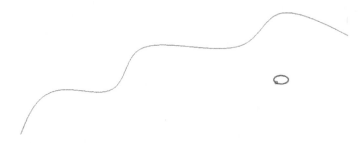

Step 3: Select sweep path.

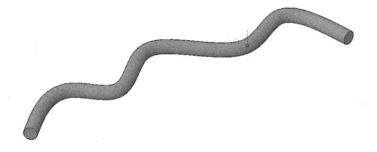

Chapter-10

3D Modify tools

3D MOVE

3d move command is use to move an object along any of the 3 axises. To do that select the object first then select 3d move object and you will found all 3 axes appear, now move the object along the desired axes by clicking on that axes and provide move distance manually.

Step 1: Ribbon≻Home tab≻Modify≻3D move.

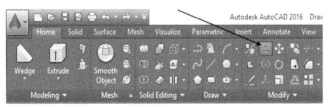

Step 2: Select object then Enter.

Step 3: Click Z Axis for Z direction move.

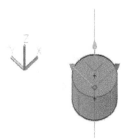

Step 4: 20 Enter for distance.

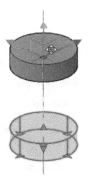

3D ROTATE

3d rotate command is use to rotate an object along any of the 3 axises. To do that, select the object first then click on 3d rotate and you see object and found all 3 axes appear, now rotate the object along desired axes by click on that axes and enter the angle manually as

More you like to rotate from an angle.

Step 1: Ribbon≻Home tab≻Modify3D rotate.

Step 2: Select object then Enter.

Step 3: Click Axis for rotate.

Step 4: 90⁰ Enter for rotate angle.

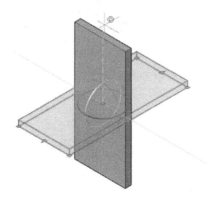

3D SCALE

3d scale command is used to scale an object along any of three (x or y or z) axis, you can change scale according to length, width or height.

Step 1: Ribbon≻Home tab≻Modify≻3D scale.

Step 2: Select object then Enter.

Step 3: Click base point.

Step 4: Pick axis.

Step 5: R Enter for reference option.

Step 6: 1 Enter for reference length.

Step 7: 2 Enter for new length.

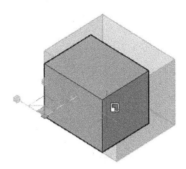

3D MIRROR

3D mirror command is used to create reflection or mirror object. But 3d mirror is different than Mirror, we can also mirror an object along z axis.

Step 1: Ribbon ➤Home tab ➤Modify ➤3D mirror.

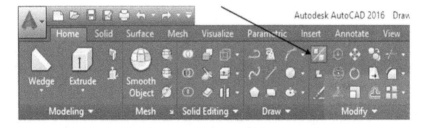

Step 2: Select object then Enter.

Step 3: Click first base point.

Step 4: Click second point.

Step 5: Click third point.

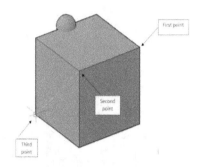

Step 6: N Enter for No, delete source object.

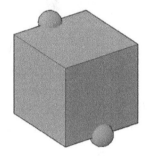

3D ARRAY

3D array command is used to create multiple copy of an object simultaneously along all of 3 axis.

Step 1: 3d array Enter.

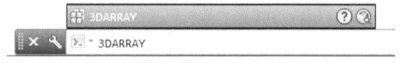

Step 2: Select object then Enter.

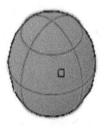

Step 3: R Enter for rectangular option.

Step 4: 5 Enter for Rows number.

Step 5: 4 Enter for Columns number.

Step 6: 3 Enter for Levels number.

Step 7: 30 Enter for distance between rows.

Step 8: 30 Enter for distance between columns.

Step 9: 30 Enter for distance between levels.

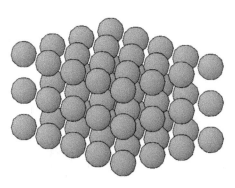

SUBTRACT

Subtract command is used to cut the intersected part of the overlapping 3d object,

For example, if you have to make a circular hole in a box then you have to intersect an object of similar radius then subtract it.

Step 1: Ribbon ➤Home tab ➤Solid editing ➤Subtract.

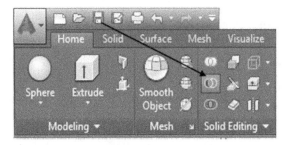

Step 2: Select first object then Enter.

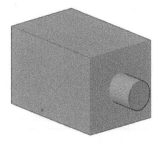

Step 3: Select second object.

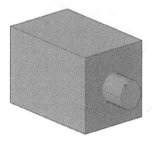

Step 4: Then Enter.

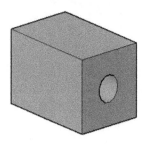

UNION

Union command is use to joint or merge two or more than two 3d object. By applying this command all participated object are seems as a block.

Step 1: Ribbon ➤Home tab ➤Solid editing ➤Union.

Step 2: Select first object.

Step 3: Select second object.

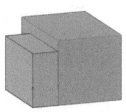

Step 4: Then Enter.

INTERSECT

Intersect command is use to cut the rest part (i.e. except intersected part) of two 3d object who is intersecting each other.

Step 1: Ribbon ➤Home tab ➤Solid editing ➤Intersect.

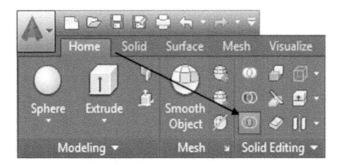

Step 2: Select first object.

Step 3: Select second object.

Step 4: Then Enter.

SLICE

Slice command is use to cut an 3d Object, and remove the isolated part.

Step 1: Ribbon ≻Home tab ≻Solid editing ≻Slice.

Step 2: Select object then Press Enter.

Step 3: Pick first point.

Step 4: Pick second point.

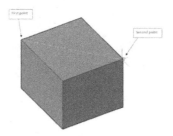

Step 5: Specify a point on desired side.

FILLET EDGE

Step 1: RibbonSolidSolid editingFillet Edge.

Step 2: Select edge then Press Enter.

Step 3: R Enter for radius option.

Step 4: Enter for fillet radius then Press Enter.

CHAMFER EDGE

Step 1: RibbonSolid ➤Solid editing ➤Chamfer Edge.

Step 2: Select edge then Press Enter.

Step 3: D Enter for distance option.

Step 4: 2 Enter for base distance.

Step 5: 2 Enter for other distance then double Enter.

Chapter-11

3D Surface & Mesh

NETWORK

A network surface can be created between a network of curves or between the edges of other 3D surfaces or solids.

Step 1: Ribbon ➤Surface ➤Create ➤Network.

Step 2: Select all first direction edges then Press Enter.

Step 3: Select all second direction edges then Press Enter.

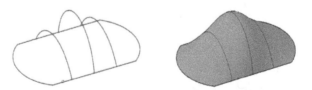

PLANAR

Create planar surfaces in the space between edge sub objects splines and other 2D and 3D curve.

With PLANESURF, planar surfaces can be created from multiple closed objects and the edges of surface or solid objects. During creation, you can specify the tangency and bulge magnitude.

Step 1: Ribbon ➤Surface ➤Create ➤Planar.

Step 2: O Enter for object option.

Step 3: Select object then Press Enter.

SURFACE BLEND

Creates a continuous blend surface between two existing surfaces.

Step 1: Ribbon ➤Surface ➤Create ➤Blend.

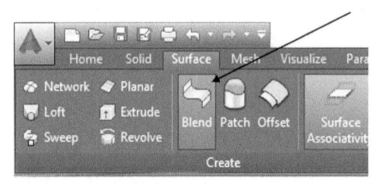

Step 2: Select first edge then Press Enter.

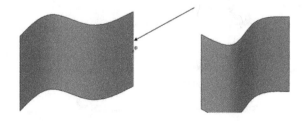

Step 3: Select second edge then Press Enter.

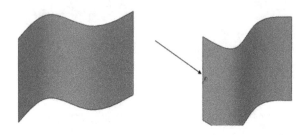

Step 4: Enter.

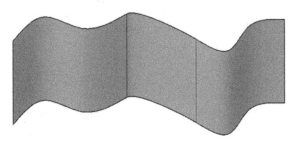

PATCH

Creates a new surface by fitting a cap over a surface edge that forms a closed loop.

Step 1: Ribbon ➢Surface ➢Create ➢Patch.

Step 2: Select surface edge.

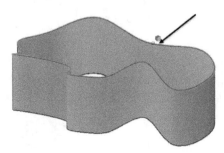

Step 3: Double Enter.

SURFACE OFFSET

Create a parallel surface or solid by setting an offset distance from a surface.

Step 1: Ribbon ➤Surface ➤Create ➤Offset.

Step 2: Select Object then enter.

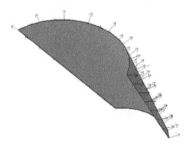

Step 3: 0.1 Enter for offset distance.

SURFACE EXTEND

Step 1:   Ribbon ≻Surface ≻Edit ≻Extend.

Step 2:   Select surface edge then enter.

Step 3:   10 Enter for extend distance.

SURFACE TRIM

Step 1:   Ribbon ≻Surface ≻Edit ≻Trim.

Step 2: Select surface then enter.

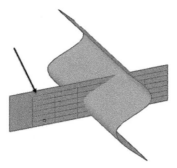

Step 3: Select cutting curves then enter.

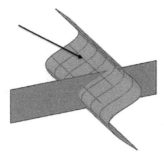

Step 4: Select area to trim.

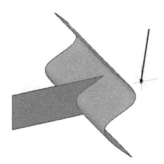

SURFACE FILLET

Step 1: Ribbon ➤Surface ➤Edit ➤Fillet.

Step 2: Select first surface.

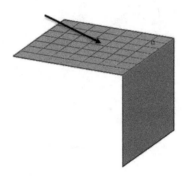

Step 3: Select second surface.

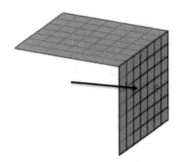

Step 4: R Enter for radius option.

Step 5: 0.5 Enter for radius then again enter.

Chapter-12

What Are The New Features Introduced in AutoCAD 2018?

REVISION CLOUD

Step 1: Revcloud Enter.

Step 2: Then R enter for rectangle shape of Revision cloud.

or

Penter for Polygon shape Revision cloud.

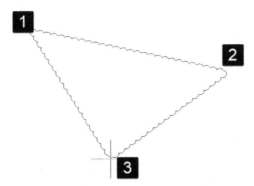

SMART DIMENSION

To measure the diameter of a circle as to measure the length of a line; two different tools are required for the same,. But with the help of smart dimension's new feature both types of dimension's can be measure with the same tool.

I.e. Smart dimension.

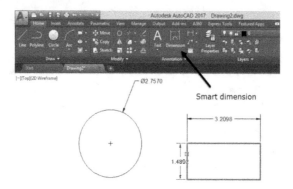

Smart dimension

GEOMETRIC CENTER (OSNAP)

Geometric any Polygon center point of it is to show. These new features are Object snapping (Osnap).

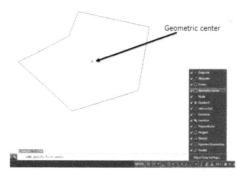

Geometric center

CENTER MARKS AND CENTER LINES

Step 1: Click Annotate tab.

Step 2: Click Center lines.

Step 3: Select first line.

Step 4: Select second line.

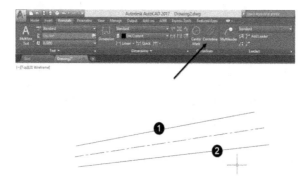

Or

Click center mark then Select circle.

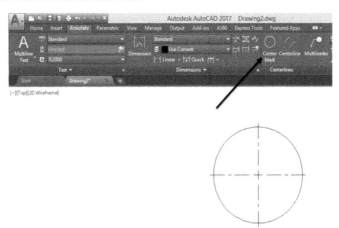

PDF file import

Step 1: Click Insert tab then click Pdf import.

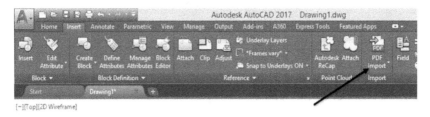

Step 2: Then enter or right click.

Step 3: Select file and open.

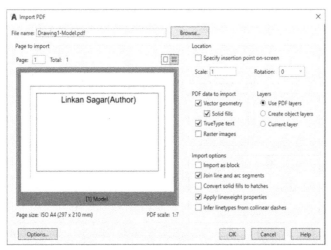

Step 4: Select scale, Rotation angle and ok.

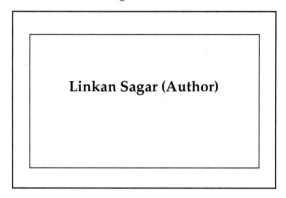

2D Practice drawing

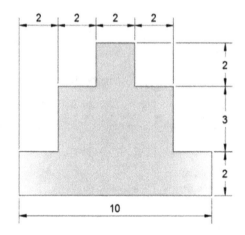

2D Practice drawing

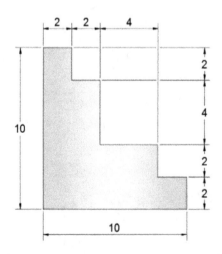

PRACTICE DRAWINGS

2D Practice drawing

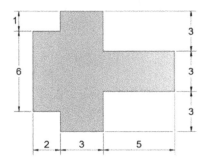

2D Practice drawing

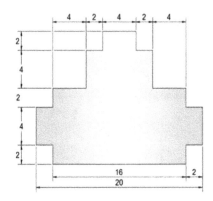

2D Practice drawing

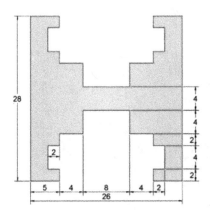

2D Practice drawing

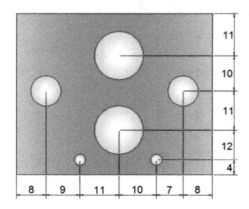

2D Practice drawing

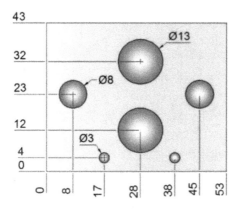

2D Practice drawing

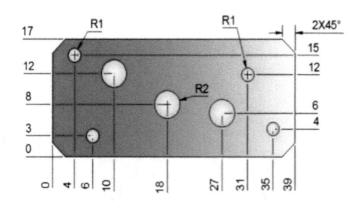

2D Practice drawing

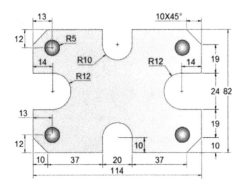

2D Practice drawing

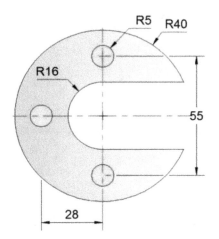

2D Practice drawing

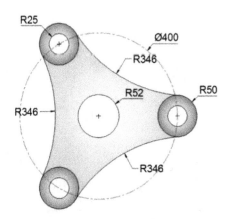

2D Practice drawing

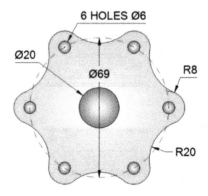

2D Practice drawing

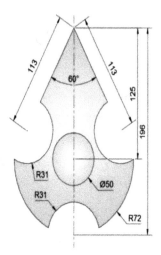

2D Practice drawing

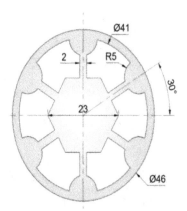

2D Practice drawing

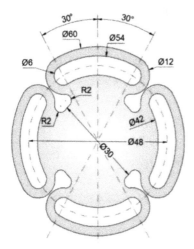

2D Practice drawing

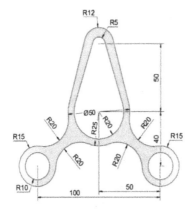

2D Practice drawing

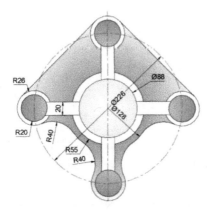

2D Practice drawing

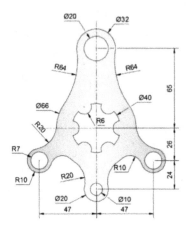

2D Practice drawing

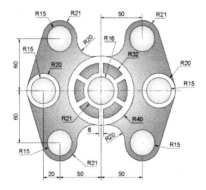

2D Practice drawing

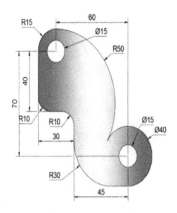

2D Practice drawing

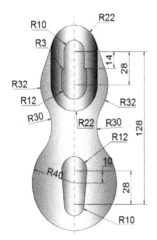

2D Practice drawing

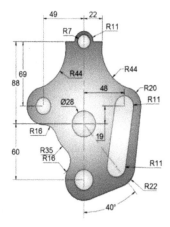

2D Practice drawing

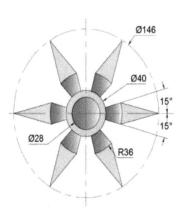

2D Practice drawing

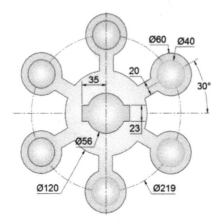

2D Practice drawing

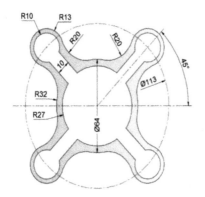

2D Practice drawing

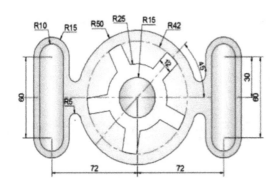

2D Practice drawing

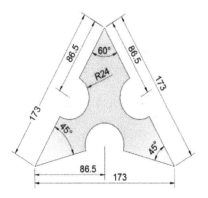

2D Practice drawing

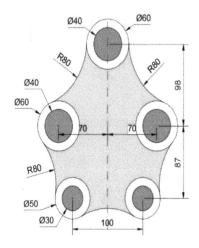

2D Practice drawing

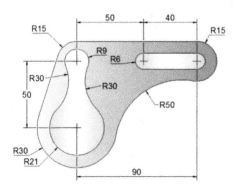

2D Practice drawing

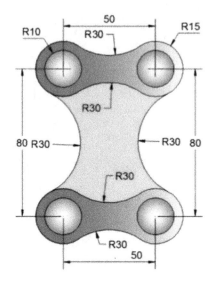

2D Practice drawing

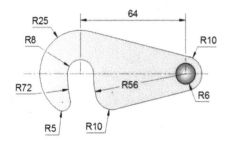

2D Practice drawing

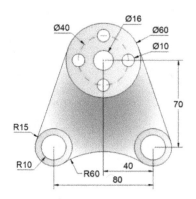

2D Practice drawing

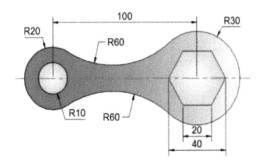

2D Practice drawing

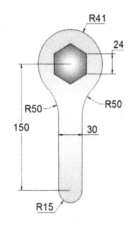

2D Practice drawing

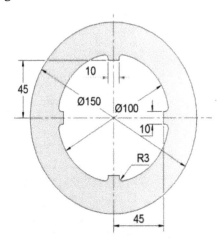

2D Practice drawing

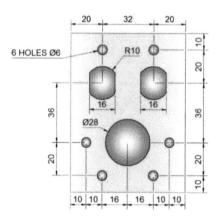

2D Practice drawing

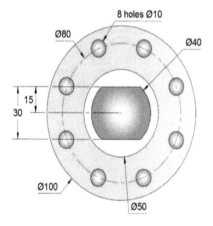

2D Practice drawing

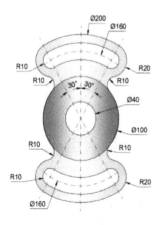

2D Practice drawing

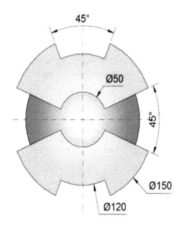

2D Practice drawing

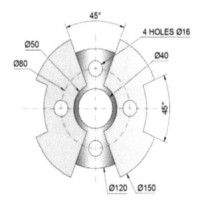

2D Practice drawing

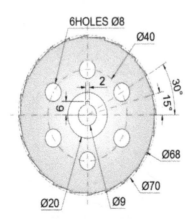

2D Practice drawing

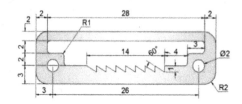

2D Practice drawing

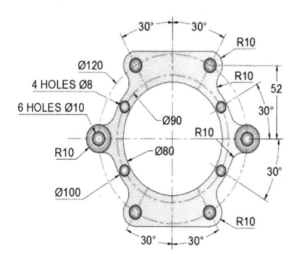

2D Practice drawing

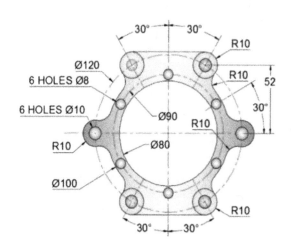

2D Practice drawing

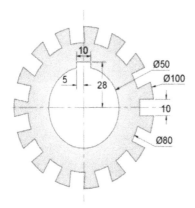

2D Practice drawing

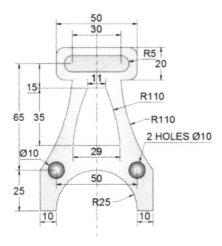

2D Practice drawing

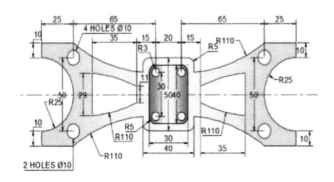

2D Practice drawing

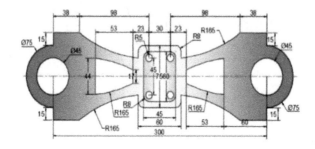

2D Practice drawing

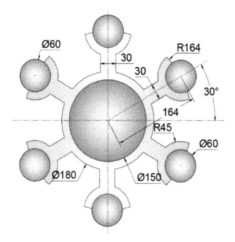

2D Practice drawing

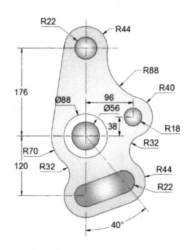

2D Practice drawing

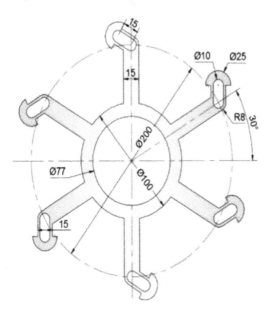

2D Practice drawing

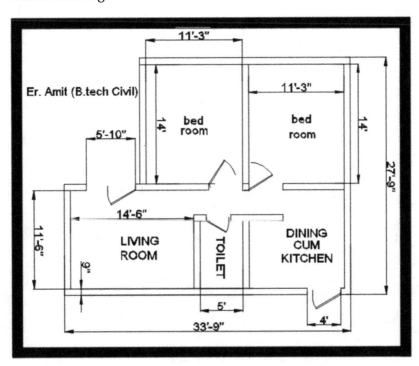

2D Practice drawing

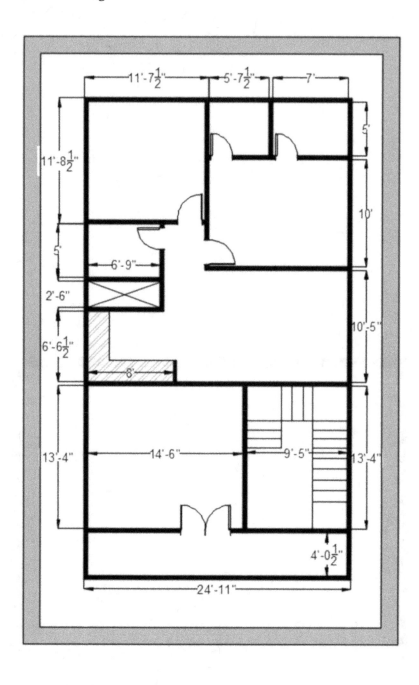

2D Practice drawing

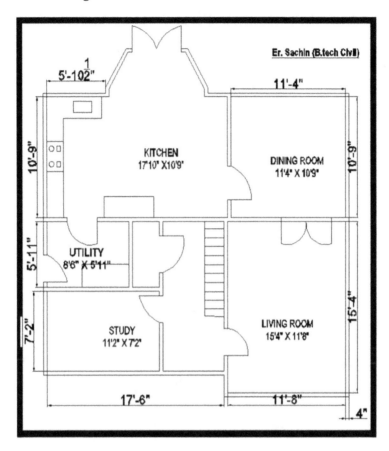

3D Practice drawing

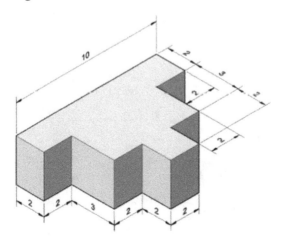

3D Practice drawing

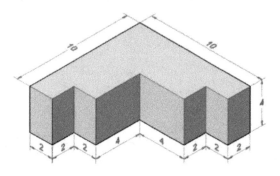

3D Practice drawing

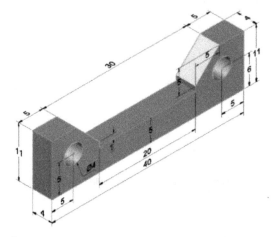

3D Practice drawing

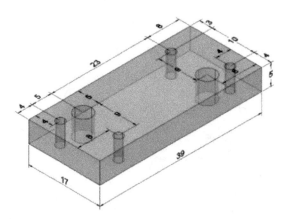

3D Practice drawing

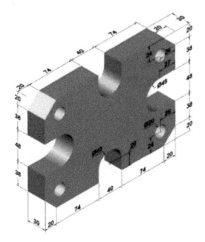

3D Practice drawing

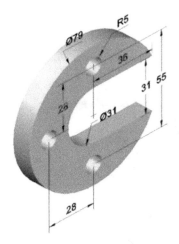

3D Practice drawing

3D Practice drawing

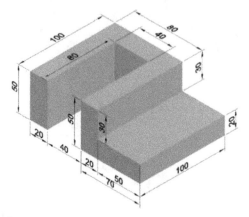

3D Practice drawing

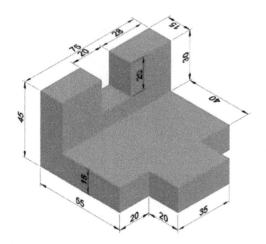

3D Practice drawing

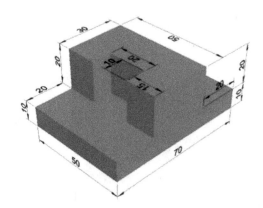

3D Practice drawing

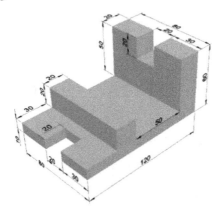

3D Practice drawing

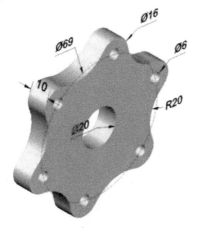

3D Practice drawing

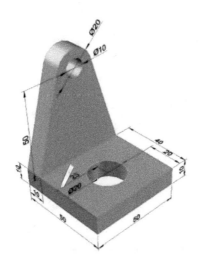

3D Practice drawing

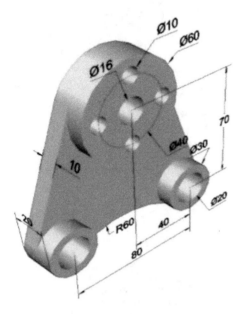

3D Practice drawing

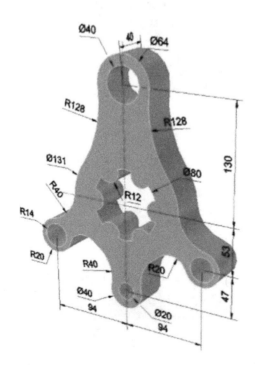